MORAL THEOLOGY

Other Books By Charles E. Curran

Christian Morality Today
A New Look at Christian Morality
Contemporary Problems in Moral Theology
Catholic Moral Theology in Dialogue
The Crisis in Priestly Ministry
Politics, Medicine and Christian Ethics:
    A Dialogue with Paul Ramsey
New Perspectives in Moral Theology
Ongoing Revision in Moral Theology
Themes in Fundamental Moral Theology
Issues in Sexual and Medical Ethics
Transition and Tradition in Moral Theology
Dissent in and for the Church *(Charles E. Curran et al.)*
The Responsibility of Dissent: The Church and Academic
    Freedom *(John F. Hunt and Terrence R. Connelly with Charl*
    E. Curran et al.)
Absolutes in Moral Theology? *(editor)*
Contraception: Authority and Dissent *(editor)*
Readings in Moral Theology No. 1: Moral Norms and
    Catholic Tradition *(coeditor with Richard A. McCormick)*
Readings in Moral Theology No. 2: The Distinctiveness of
    Christian Ethics *(coeditor with Richard A. McCormick)*
Readings in Moral Theology No. 3: The Magisterium and
    Morality *(coeditor with Richard A. McCormick)*

Moral Theology:
A Continuing Journey

CHARLES E. CURRAN

UNIVERSITY OF NOTRE DAME PRESS
NOTRE DAME - LONDON

196442

Library of Congress Cataloging in Publication Data

Curran, Charles E.
  Moral theology, a continuing journey

  Includes bibliographical references and index.
  Contents: The context of moral theology: Theology,
hierarchical magisterium and church. Catholic theology
and academe—Methodological questions: A methodological
overview of fundamental moral theology. Three issues
in methodology—Personal ethics: A theological perspective on aging— [etc.]
  1. Christian ethics—Catholic authors. I. Title.
BJ1249.C818   241′.042   81-23160
ISBN 0-268-01350-0   AACR2
ISBN 0-268-01351-9 (pbk.)

To my sister Kay
With gratitude

Contents

Acknowledgments

Many people have contributed to my own continuing journey of doing moral theology. I particularly want to thank Richard Miller for his assistance in preparing this volume and Patricia Whitlow for typing most of the manuscript. Johann Klodzen, Sally Ann McReynolds, and Cindi Vian also helped. Bruce Miller and his associates in the Theology Library of The Catholic University of America, David Gilson and Alan Flood, have continued to be of assistance. Daphne Burt has prepared the index for the volume.

I am grateful to the following institutions and societies for the opportunity to give lectures and papers which in a later and revised form now appear in this volume: the Department of Theology of the University of Notre Dame; the National Catholic School of Social Service of The Catholic University of America; the Ethics Advisory Board of the Department of Health, Education, and Welfare; the Society of Health and Human Values; the Philosophy Department of the University of Santa Clara; the Law School of New York University.

Finally I appreciatively acknowledge the permission of the following periodicals and publishers for allowing me to use in this volume materials which appeared in their publications: *America*, for "Theology, Hierarchical Magisterium, and Church"; *The Furrow*, for "Catholic Theology and Academe"; *Studia Moralia*, for "A Methodological Overview of Fundamental Moral Theology"; the University of Notre Dame, for "Three Issues in Methodology"; *Social Thought*, for "A Theological Per-

spective on Aging"; the Ethics Advisory Board of the
Department of Health, Education, and Welfare, for *"In
Vitro* Fertilization and Embryo Transfer"; *The American
Journal of Theology and Philosophy,* for "The Contra-
ceptive Revolution and the Human Condition"; *The
Thomist,* for "The Changing Anthropological Bases of
Catholic Social Ethics"; and *The Jurist* for "Religion,
Law, and Public Policy in America."

Introduction

The nine chapters in this book originally appeared as individual studies of various aspects of moral theology. No attempt has been made to make these studies part of an artificially created whole. However, the pilgrim and historical character of moral theology is a unifying thread running throughout these pages.

All contemporary theology is marked by historical consciousness. Gone is an older classicism which saw truth in terms of the eternal, the immutable, and the unchanging. The historical character of moral theology is especially evident, for moral theology deals with the ways in which Christians should act and respond to the changing world in which we live. The historical character of moral theology recognizes both continuity and discontinuity with the past, for the ongoing quest of moral theology does not jettison the past but tries to build creatively on the past in the light of the present. The chapters brought together in this book illustrate this continuing journey of moral theology.

Part one discusses the context of moral theology. The relationship of theology to the total church and to the hierarchical magisterium has been a most sensitive issue. As is seen in chapter one, the relationship between the hierarchical magisterium and theology is quite complex and cannot be reduced to a totally one-sided dependence or independence of the theological enterprise. It is precisely the historical nature of Christian faith and of Christian theology which adds to the complexity of the relationship. Theology must continually search for better understandings of God and of the Christian response in the light of the changing realities of our existence. It will never be sufficient for the total church and the hierarchical church merely to repeat the past formulations. Theology by its very nature plays the role of the scout who goes ahead to explore the terrain; understanding of the faith depends upon such theological advances. However, theology must always remain faithful to the Word of God as revealed in the scriptures and lived in tradition which is proclaimed by the official teachers in the church.

A second important context for all theology refers to the place in which theology exists. As one looks back on history, theology has been most creative when it has flourished in a university setting. The American academy has throughout this century developed the protections and safeguards necessary for the intellectual pursuit of truth. Chapter two attempts to show that the American understanding of academic freedom proposes the best practical solution for maintaining both the creativity and the fidelity of Catholic theology. The church and theology will be best served by recognizing and accepting the practice of academic freedom as it has been developed in the American context. However, at the present time official Catholic leadership shows a great resistance to taking this significant historical step.

Part two of the book discusses methodological questions. Moral theology until the last two decades seemed static and unchanging. Now there is much ferment and search for more satisfying approaches. The methodological overview of fundamental moral theology proposed in chapter three attempts to present an outline of the way in which the discipline should be developed. Such an approach recognizes the need to be faithful both to the past insights of our tradition and to the needs of the contemporary time. Methodological questions such as the nature of the discipline itself, anthropology, and the matter of a distinctively Christian morality and ethics are perennial topics, but these questions must be raised anew in the light of contemporary developments. Our understanding of anthropology, for example, has changed a good deal, especially in the light of our consciousness of historicity. The issue of a distinctively Christian morality and ethics came to the fore with the shift from a natural law approach to a more explicitly biblical and Christian understanding of moral theology.

Part three discusses three questions in personal ethics— aging, *in vitro* fertilization, and the contraceptive revolution. These considerations illustrate why the historical character of moral theology is even more pronounced than that of other parts of systematic theology. Moral theology deals with actions, and new questions and problems are always arising. Aging has been a constant reality in human existence, but the meaning and the programmatic ways of dealing with aging have never been more intensely studied and discussed. *In vitro* fertilization and contraception are two significant modern developments that stem from the new biology. The historical character of moral theology in no way denies continuity with the past. Historicity properly recognizes both continuity and discontinuity. To address these questions properly a Christian anthropology is most important. Our past understanding of Christian anthropology enables us to shed much light on these matters, but the historical character of moral theology reminds us that the consideration of these issues also gives us a better understanding of Christian anthropology. The solutions proposed in this section illustrate the need to be both critical and appreciative of historical developments.

Part four includes two studies on social ethics. The first considers the historical development involved in official Catholic social teaching from the late nineteenth century of Pope Leo XIII to the present day. Before the Second Vatican Council the historical character of theology was neglected. However, a closer examination of this body of official Catholic teaching indicates great historical development. Unfortunately, many of the commentators dealing with Catholic social teaching failed to recognize this historical character and the need for an historical hermeneutic in interpreting such teaching. The acceptance of modern tools of biblical studies led the Catholic Church to recognize the historical character of the scriptures and the need for hermeneutics. This recognition now extends to the interpretation of the official magisterial teaching of the church. Chapter eight concentrates on the changing anthropological bases in official Catholic teaching and tries to explain how and why development occurred toward an insistence on freedom, equality, and participation together with a greater appreciation of the social nature of persons and of human reality.

The last chapter studies the always important question of the relationship of faith and religion to the political order. The historical context of this study is the contemporary American scene in the light of discussions about abortion and the New Christian Right. Too often editorialists give simplistic answers to these complex questions. This chapter recognizes the complex relationship between the political order and the religious and moral orders. The proposed criterion of political purpose safeguards both the integrity of the political order and governs the way in which faith and religion can try to affect the political order.

The chapters in this book thus touch on the four major concerns of moral theology—the ecclesial and academic contexts of moral theology, methodology, personal ethics, and social ethics. But above all, these studies indicate and illustrate the historical character of moral theology. Moral theology involves a continuing journey.

PART ONE

The Context of Moral Theology

1. Theology, Hierarchical Magisterium, and Church

Recent investigations of prominent Roman Catholic theologians have once again focused attention on the possibility of heresy in the church and how to deal with it. The present cases will serve to limit the discussion to the question of the role and function of theology vis-a-vis the role and function of the hierarchical magisterium in the Catholic Church.

The contemporary episodes also show that the question is broader than heresy. Heresy in the strict sense of the term is the denial of a truth proposed by the church as revealed. Many of the tensions in the life of the church today between the hierarchical magisterium and theologians do not concern the revealed truths of faith, no matter how this term is understood. Discussions about moral issues such as contraception and sterilization or the possibility of dissent from authoritative, noninfallible teachings of the hierarchical magisterium on moral matters do not involve heresy in the strict sense of the term. What is opposed to church teaching which is not proposed as revealed is technically called "error" in the manuals of theology.

One other important limitation comes from the present circumstances. Although the issues under discussion often involve defined truths of faith, all admit that the investigations of theologians have not involved the infallible teaching office of the church. Consequently, our consideration will purposely prescind from the whole question of infallibility in church teaching.

3

It is impossible and unnecessary to repeat here the discussions in contemporary theology about the relationship between the God-given function of the hierarchical magisterium and the role of theology in the church. The crux of the problem is accurately posed in the following question: Does the authoritative hierarchical magisterium always constitute the only factor or the always decisive factor in the total magisterial activity of the church?

In my judgment both history and many contemporary theologians answer the question in the negative. The very term "the authoritative hierarchical magisterium," which is often used today, only came into existence in the nineteenth century. More importantly, history shows instances of errors in hierarchical teaching which were later corrected, at least partially due to theological dissent.

Theologically, the teaching function of the church as such is broader than the teaching function of the hierarchical church. All share in the task of understanding better the gospel message. Through baptism all Christians share in the prophetic and teaching office of Jesus and possess the gift of the Spirit. An analogy can be made with the different kinds of sharing in the priesthood of Jesus. An important theological basis for the growth of the liturgical movement in Catholicism before the Second Vatican Council came from the recognition that all Christians share in the priestly function of Jesus. The priesthood of all believers exists together with the hierarchical priesthood. In the same way all share in some way in the teaching function of Jesus, but there is also the hierarchical teaching office. The teaching function of the church is not totally identical with the hierarchical teaching office. There can be no absolute division between the hierarchy as the teaching church and the rest of the faithful as the learning church.

In this perspective it is false to see the total question only in terms of the relationship between the hierarchical teaching office and the role of theologians. The whole church and all the faithful share in some way in the magisterial function of the church. However, our practical concerns limit the discussion to the narrower question of the relationship between the hierarchical teaching office and theologians.

The theological function is to understand and interpret the reality of the Christian mystery in the world in which we live. Theology has a creative and a critical function. However, theology is limited or governed, to employ the strongest but perhaps not the most accurate terms, by the "authorities" of faith—scripture and tradition which are interpreted by the God-given hierarchical teaching function in the church. There are limits on what constitutes Catholic theology. Heresy and error are possible.

The hierarchical teaching office proclaims, makes creatively present, and safeguards the Christian faith. To carry out its mission, the episcopal and papal office must be in touch with the experience of the faithful and the teaching of theologians. However, that teaching office (prescinding from the whole matter of infallibility) can be wrong in its teachings and judgments despite the presumptions in its favor based on the gift of the Spirit. In addition, the hierarchical magisterium, in carrying out its mission, uses theology. For all practical purposes there is no such thing as a pure proclamation of faith without any help of theology. All recognize that the documents proposed by the hierarchical magisterium and the teachings of popes and councils have also involved the collaboration of theology in one way or another.

The role of theology is not totally absorbed into or entirely subordinated to the hierarchical magisterium, but theology must give due weight to the authoritative hierarchical teachings. Yes, errors and heresy are possible in theology. Yes, the hierarchical teaching office has a God-given role to protect the church from heresy. But in making such judgments the hierarchical teaching office is somewhat dependent on theology and, in all but its most solemn statements, is subject to the possibility of error. Here is the rub.

The problem of the possibility of error and even heresy in theology is not a new one. The Catholic Church can and should learn from its own history in this matter. Since the time of the Counter-Reformation, Roman Catholicism has stressed the authority of the church in the historical struggles in which it was engaged. In the nineteenth-century struggle against Continental liberalism, with its emphasis on the autonomy of conscience and the omnicompetency of the state, Catholicism emphasized the authority of God and of the church.

This stress on authority also colored the exercise of the teaching office in the church in general and its attitudes toward theologians in particular. The authoritarian reaction to modernism in the twentieth century saw the unfortunate silencing of significant theological voices such as LaGrange. This overly authoritarian approach was very evident in the 1950s. The encyclical *Humani generis* condemned the *nouvelle théologie* and declared that whenever the pope goes out of his way to speak on a controverted issue, the subject is no longer a matter for free debate among theologians. (The Second Vatican Council expressly rejected that same sentence.) The theologians Chenu and Congar, de Lubac and Teilhard de Chardin, John Courtney Murray and others were silenced and restricted in their teaching and writing.

The Second Vatican Council brought about dramatic changes. Many of the silenced theologians of the 1950s were the architects of the new teachings of the council. The ecclesiology of the council described the church as the people of God and the pilgrim church in reaction to an older, overly authoritarian approach, which saw the church primarily as a hierarchical society with a pyramid structure.

However, there are many indications that these startling changes have not been totally incorporated into the life and structure of the church. One example concerns the paternalistic and authoritarian manner in which the hierarchical officeholders often view and treat the people of God.

In an address to Catholic academics during his visit to the United States in 1979, Pope John Paul II discussed the same basic issue that we are considering. He rightly stressed the three aspects that must be considered—the academic freedom of the theologian, which is seen in relationship to the finality of the academic enterprise, the role of the hierarchical teaching office, and the rights of the people of God. A lay colleague sitting next to me was quite disturbed by his treatment of the people of God. "It is the right of the faithful not to be troubled by theories and hypotheses that they are not expert in judging or that are easily simplified or manipulated by public opinion." To my friend this smacked of treating the people of God as the illiterate masses.

Too often we worry about protecting the weak and the scandal that might be given to them. What about the scandal of the strong? Many intelligent lay Catholics would be scandalized if Catholic theologians were not searching for better understandings and proposing new theories. Look at the number who have left the church because the Christian message seems to be no longer meaningful for them in their world. At the very least there are both weak and strong in the church. Too often authority in the church acts as if all the people of God were dumb sheep or illiterate masses who must be directed from without in all they do.

Another aspect of the historical context is also very important—the changing nature of theology itself. Older approaches dealing with theological error and heresy were based not only on an overly authoritarian view of the hierarchical magisterium but also on a particular understanding of theology itself.

Many commentators have pointed to the shift from classicism to historical mindedness as the underlying explanation of the changes in theology found in the Second Vatican Council. Classicism stressed the eternal, the immutable, and the unchanging. This approach sought a universal, abstract way of knowing which was fundamentally applicable in all times and circumstances. Historical and temporal realities only brought about accidental differences. Historical consciousness gives greater importance to the particular, the individual, the historical, and the changing.

The aim of the Second Vatican Council was to make the

word and work of God more meaningful to the world and situation in which we live. Merely to repeat and apply the formulas and understandings of the past was not sufficient. On the basis of a thorough knowledge of the past, theology has the function to make the Christian mystery an appealing and living reality in our world. As a corollary, the judgment of orthodoxy cannot be based merely on the verbal adherence to the formulas or understanding of an older theology, for different formulas and understandings might be required today. The role of theology thus becomes more significant, more creative, and more perilous.

The historical consciousness underlying much of Vatican II theology has further ramifications. In the last decades more emphasis has been given to theology as reflection on the experience of the Christian community. But experience differs in accord with the concrete cultural and social life of the people. As a result there can be a legitimate theological diversity in different cultural settings. Catholic thinkers accepting such historical mindedness naturally are opposed to any total relativity of truth.

The emphasis on praxis in much of contemporary theology well illustrates this point. This same aspect of historical consciousness is also recognized in the 1971 Apostolic Letter *Octogesima adveniens* of Pope Paul VI.

> In the face of such widely varying situations it is difficult for us to utter a unified message and to put forward a solution which has universal validity. Such is not our ambition, nor is it our mission. It is up to the Christian communities to analyze with objectivity the situation which is proper to their own country, to shed on it the light of the Gospel's unalterable words and to draw principles of reflection, norms of judgment and directives for action from the social teaching of the Church (par. 4).

In the light of the historical contexts of an overly authoritarian approach by the hierarchical church in the past and of a shift to historical consciousness in theology, both the role of the hierarchical teaching office and the function of theology have become more complex. The episcopal and papal teaching office includes much more than the judicial function of determining when heresy and error are present. Above all, their role is positive and supporting—to proclaim the gospel and to encourage all in the church to make the truths of faith creatively present in word and deed in our world. To stimulate the creative fidelity of theological endeavor is an important aspect of the episcopal function.

The primary responsibility for avoiding error and even possible heresy in theology rests with the individual theologian and the theological community. The faith, competence, integrity, and responsibility of the individual theological scholar require that the Catholic theologian truly be such. The theological community as any community of scholars has the obligation to be rigorously critical in assessing the work of colleagues without engaging in personal attacks of any kind. The discipline of theology contains this built-in mechanism of critical dialogue to safeguard its own integrity and fidelity.

The hierarchical teaching office does have a judicial function concerning error and possible heresy in theology, but in the light of all that has been pointed out above, the advice of Gamaliel should be taken very seriously (Acts 5:34-41). At times it might be necessary for the hierarchical teaching office to intervene, but interventions by the hierarchical teaching office about the teachings of a particular theologian should have a "last resort" quality about them.

I suggest three other considerations to guide any judicial intervention by the hierarchical teaching office. First, the interventions of the hierarchical magisterium themselves always involve and employ some theological approach. Theologians collaborating with the hierarchical teaching office in this particular function should be truly representative of all Catholic theology and not just of one particular school. Second, the emphasis on experience and praxis in the light of cultural differences, together with a greater recognition of the importance of the local church, indicates that these interventions should first take place at the more local level. Third, the procedures must incorporate all the recognized due process safeguards in order to protect the rights of the theologians involved.

History indicates that there has always been a tension in the church between the theological enterprise and the episcopal and papal teaching office. An understanding of both roles comes to the same conclusion. Such tension can be creative and not destructive if there is an atmosphere of mutual trust and respect. Such an atmosphere is much more important than any process or procedure.

The future of the church will be best served if the current climate of suspicion, distrust, and fear on both sides can be changed. One possible way to improve the present situation would be for the hierarchical teaching office and the theological community to collaborate in working out the procedures that should be employed if the hierarchical magisterium prudently comes to the conclusion that some judicial intervention is necessary.

2. Catholic Theology and Academe

Freedom has been a perennial topic of discussion in Catholic thought. Ever fearful of individualistic license and of the dangers of denying an objective morality based on the law of God, Roman Catholic theology in the nineteenth century opposed the modern freedoms—freedom of worship, freedom of speech, of teaching, of the press and freedom of conscience. However, in the last few decades the Roman Catholic Church has become a staunch defender of human dignity and of human freedom. In the light of this changing emphasis of freedom the Second Vatican Council accepted religious liberty for all peoples. Discussions about academic freedom took place in the context of this developing attitude toward freedom in general and toward the concrete manifestations of freedom.

The purpose of this study is to examine the relationship between academic freedom, the Catholic university, and Roman Catholic theology. The topic seems quite limited, but actually there are many significant questions connected with this topic which can only be presented in a summary fashion. This study will consist of four parts: (I) the meaning of academic freedom; (II) the relationship of the Catholic university to academic freedom; (III) Roman Catholic theology and academic freedom; (IV) academic freedom as related to *Sapientia christiana,* the recent Apostolic Constitution on norms for ecclesiastical universities and faculties, and also to the proposed new code of canon law.

I. Meaning of Academic Freedom

Academic freedom is related to all other aspects of freedom, but what specifies academic freedom is its relationship to the university. The university in this context is generally understood to include all institutions of higher learning such as undergraduate colleges and universities. A university exists to preserve, impart, and discover truth. To achieve its purpose the university as a community of scholars needs a proper academic environment. Academic freedom is essential for the very existence of a university and is what distinguishes a university from a propaganda institution or a center of indoctrination. The university as such must be a free and autonomous center of study with no external constraints limiting either its autonomy or its freedom. An often-cited definition of academic freedom is the following:

> Academic freedom is the freedom of the teacher or research worker in higher institutions of learning to investigate and discuss the problems of his science and to express his conclusions, whether through publication or in the instruction of students, without interference from political or ecclesiastical authority, or from the administrative officials of the institution in which he is employed, unless his methods are found by qualified bodies of his own profession to be clearly incompetent or contrary to professional ethics.[1]

Academic freedom is based not on the personal privilege of academics but on the common good of society. Society is best served by institutions of higher learning in which there is a free search for truth and free expression. The only limit is the truth itself and nothing else. Academic freedom applies to the teaching, research, and extramural utterances of the professor. The teacher is to be guided only by truth and its understanding. The integrity of the faculty member and the rights of the students are violated if the teacher is not allowed to express one's own ideas and hypotheses based on scientific knowledge and investigation. Freedom in research is fundamental to the advancement of all knowledge. Nor can a faculty member's freedom be summarily taken away because of controversial extramural utterances which might upset some of the different publics served by the university. However, the right of academic freedom carries with it corresponding duties. In general, the right to freedom involves the duty to use that freedom responsibly. More specifically in terms of academic freedom, the individual professor's responsibility is spelled out in terms of competency and integrity as a teacher and researcher.

The concept of academic freedom briefly described here has been developed in the United States in the light of historical circumstances and of the growth of higher education. One of the functions of a university is to be critical, but in the process influential and powerful people might be upset by such criticism or new hypotheses. Problems have arisen in many different subject areas including religion, science, history, politics, economics, sexual ethics, business, and race.[2]

In the United States the work of developing and spelling out the procedures and institutions needed to protect the autonomy of the university and academic freedom has been done especially by the American Association of University Professors (AAUP). It should be pointed out that structures and procedures are the minimal safeguards needed to protect academic freedom. A vigorous intellectual community with highly competent and dedicated scholars cannot be brought about through legal procedures alone. At the time of the founding of the AAUP in 1915 a committee on academic freedom and tenure formulated "A Declaration of Principles" which set forth the concerns of the association for academic freedom, tenure, proper procedures, and professional responsibilities. From a meeting called by the American Council on Education in 1925 there emerged the "Conference Statement on Academic Freedom and Tenure," which because of its endorsement by the Association of American Colleges and by the AAUP was quite generally supported within American higher education. This somewhat unwieldy statement of rules and regulations designed to be incorporated by institutions of higher learning was replaced in 1940 by a set of principles approved by both associations and known as the "1940 Statement of Principles on Academic Freedom and Tenure." This statement, which has been endorsed by the most significant academic associations, is generally accepted as governing higher education in the United States. The AAUP has also issued further statements and proposed regulations based on the 1940 statement, especially the "1958 Statement on Procedural Standards in Faculty Dismissal Proceedings" and the "1976 Recommended Institutional Regulations on Academic Freedom and Tenure." In addition to its work of proposing principles and regulations the AAUP also investigates alleged violations of academic freedom, trying to work out amicable solutions in accord with its principles, but at times having to take the more drastic action of censuring institutions which violate the principles of academic freedom.[3]

The two instrumentalities designed to protect academic freedom are tenure and academic due process. After a probationary period the professor is entitled to a permanent or tenured appointment if the institution decides to keep such a professor. A tenured professor can be dismissed only for adequate cause. Adequate cause is not precisely defined but certainly includes the notion of competency and the fitness to teach and do research. Although one of the purposes of tenure is to safeguard the academic freedom of the professor, full academic freedom is also demanded for faculty on probationary appointments.

Academic due process, as explained in the 1958 AAUP statement and elsewhere, spells out the procedures to be employed in attempting to dismiss a professor for adequate cause. Academic due process calls for a judgment by academic peers together with all the legal safeguards and procedures connected with due process. It is normally expected that the governing board of the institution will accept the decision of the faculty committee. In recognizing incompetency and unfitness as grounds for dismissal, this procedure legally enshrines the fundamental responsibility which is the duty of all faculty members to exercise. To dismiss a professor after incompetency has been demonstrated and recognized by a committee of peers in accord with academic due process in no way constitutes a violation of academic freedom.[4] The principles and procedures briefly described here are generally accepted by all in dealing with the meaning and actual protection of academic freedom in American higher education. Today there are some who for academic reasons want to modify or even abolish the tenure system, but they still insist on safeguarding academic freedom.

II. Catholic Higher Education and Academic Freedom

From the beginning defenders of academic freedom have been very wary of denominational institutions of higher learning. The 1915 "Declaration of Principles" firmly stated the principle that if a church establishes a college with the express understanding that the college will be used as an instrument of propaganda and indoctrination in the interests of the religious faith, such an institution does not allow academic freedom and is not truly a university. However, the declaration goes on to note that such institutions are rare and are becoming more rare. The 1940 statement recognized a problem and attempted to solve it by a general declaration that "limitations of academic freedom because of religious or other aims of the institution should be clearly stated in writing at the time of the appointment."[5]

Before the 1960s there was a widespread feeling among college and university educators in general and among Catholic leaders in these fields that the Catholic institution of higher education was incompatible with the full or absolute academic freedom existing in American institutions of higher education. Some non-Catholic educators accepted the Shavian dictum that a Catholic university is a contradiction in terms. Sidney Hook affirmed that academic freedom does not exist in Catholic institutions.[6] Robert M. MacIver, the director of the American Academic Freedom Project housed at Columbia University in the early 1950s, in his influential volume *Academic Freedom in Our Time* includes statements by Catholics to illustrate the religious line of attack on academic freedom.[7]

From the Catholic side before 1960 there was also general agreement that full academic freedom could not exist in Catholic institutions. The president of Georgetown University in 1950 referred to the sacred fetish of academic freedom and called for sensible limitations to preserve the future of the nation from fatal consequences.[8] The immediate context of his remarks was the controversy about communists and academic freedom, which was quite widespread during those years. The incompatibility between Catholic colleges and full academic freedom was accepted as a matter of course. There were very few studies of academic freedom and Catholic higher education until the 1950s. Before 1960 only one Catholic institution was censured by the AAUP for violating academic freedom, and there were no ad hoc committee reports about possible violations which did not result in censure. The two most in-depth studies of academic freedom from the Catholic perspective in the 1950s proposed an understanding of academic freedom which is opposed to and destructive of the accepted understanding in American academe. According to these studies academic freedom is limited not only by the competency and responsibility of the individual scholar but also by a specific doctrinal test of a religious nature. Ecclesiastical authority, from which there is no appeal, can by invoked to settle controverted cases in academe. One of the pedagogical functions of the teacher is to solidify and deepen the faith of the student. Loss of faith by students reflects unfavorably on a Catholic college teacher.[9]

In the 1960s great changes occurred. Catholic scholarly organizations began to endorse the 1940 statement. Faculty at Catholic institutions frequently called in the AAUP to vindicate their rights and their academic freedom. In 1965 Gerald F. Kreyche published a paper in the *National Catholic Education Association Bulletin* that called for Catholic institutions to accept the concept of full academic freedom. More favorable articles together with some dissent followed.[10] A symposium at the University of Notre Dame in 1966 heard from many speakers who saw the need for Catholic institutions of higher learning to incorporate the principle of complete academic freedom.[11] A thesis accepted at The Catholic University of America in 1969 made the case for full academic freedom even for Roman Catholic theology, a position which had been rejected in a 1958 dissertation.[12]

Perhaps the strongest indication of the extent of the changes is found in what is called the Land O'Lakes Statement "The Nature of the Contemporary Catholic University," which was signed in 1967 by twenty-six leaders in Catholic higher education in the United States and Canada, including the presidents and representatives of the major Catholic institutions. The very first paragraph states the position on academic freedom bluntly and clearly:

> The Catholic university today must be a university in the full modern sense of the word, with a strong commitment to and concern for academic excellence. To perform its teaching and research functions effectively, the Catholic university must have a true autonomy and academic freedom in the face of authority of whatever kind, lay or clerical, external to the academic community itself. To say this is simply to assert that institutional autonomy and academic freedom are essential conditions of life and growth and indeed of survival for Catholic universities as for all universities.[13]

A 1971 report of the North American Region of the International Federation of Catholic Universities (IFCU) emphasizes the need for the autonomy of the university as such. "The Catholic university is not simply a pastoral arm of the Church. It is an independent organization serving Christian purposes but not subject to ecclesiastical-juridical control, censorship or supervision." In a university without statutory relationships to Rome the hierarchical magisterium might in an extreme case issue a public warning about the theologizing activity of a particular theologian, but there can be "no question of juridical intervention in the institutional affairs of the university itself."[14]

Cultural changes included especially the general attitude of Catholics to American institutions and culture. After the Second World War the American Catholic population was being assimilated into the mainstream of American life. The church of the immigrants was moving out of the ghetto. On the one hand, the fears of some Catholics about incompatibility between Catholicism and the American ethos were greatly dissipated. On the other hand, Americans as a whole no longer looked on Catholics primarily with suspicion and mistrust. The election of a Catholic as president of the United States in 1960 symbolically indicated there was no incompatibility between Catholicism and the American ethos with its emphasis on political freedoms and human rights and its important institutions such as universities. Many Catholics matriculated at these non-Catholic institutions and did not find the environment inimical to their faith.

Since the 1950s John Tracy Ellis, Walter Ong, and Thomas O'Dea had pointed out the failure of Catholics to contribute to American intellectual life.[15] This criticism was a sign of a growing maturity that allowed Catholics to be self-critical and at the same time encouraged Catholic institutions of higher education to take a critical look at themselves.

Significant developments were occurring in Catholic higher education itself. The number of Catholic institutions and the number of students in such colleges increased dramatically after the Second World War. At the same time Catholic institutions became more interested in graduate education with its emphasis on research, investigation, and discovery. In the light of the increasing number and size of Catholic institutions, religious and clerical teachers and even administrators were supplemented by an ever-growing number of lay people, many of whom had been trained at prestigious non-Catholic schools with their strong traditions of autonomy and freedom. The same time-period saw the breakdown of the perennial philosophy-theology curriculum in Catholic colleges which attempted to hand down the classical wisdom to the new generations. Changes in governance included not only a greater role for laity in the faculty and administration but also the transfer of the ownership and incorporation of many institutions from the sponsoring religious community or group to boards of trustees which often had a majority of lay members. Catholic institutions in the 1960s experienced the same problems and questions that were present on all campuses. Even in Catholic colleges, for example, greater freedom and responsibility were given to students not only in curriculum but also in terms of their life styles on campus, for many rejected the understanding of the college as existing *in loco parentis.*

Above all, in the 1960s Catholic educators of higher learning recognized the primary purpose of their institutions was intellectual, and they should not be seen as juridically serving under and subordinate to the pastoral mission of the church. They could best serve the church by being good institutions of higher learning and holding on to their autonomy as such. Many factors contributed to this new understanding and focus: in competition with other colleges and universities Catholic institutions accepted the goal of striving for academic excellence; accrediting agencies emphasized such intellectual goals and purposes; federal and state monies were available to institutions of higher learning which did not exist primarily to carry on indoctrination; the cultural and other changes in Catholic higher education also pointed toward the primary academic and intellectual purposes of Catholic institutions.

Changing theological factors, especially as illustrated in the Second Vatican Council, also influenced the acceptance of full academic freedom as an essential aspect of Catholic colleges and universities. The Pastoral Constitution on the Church in the Modern World (nn. 36;59) affirms the legitimate autonomy of earthly affairs, created things, culture, and the sciences. All things are endowed with their own stability, truth, goodness, proper laws, and order. Catholics should not divert these realities from their own natural purposes and functions. In this perspective one can argue that the church should accept the university as it is with its own nature and purposes. The

Catholic university should not change the nature of a
university and therby violate the autonomy of the natural
or created order.

Roman Catholic theology traditionally has maintained
that faith and reason cannot contradict one another.
According to both the Pastoral Constitution on the
Church in the Modern World (n. 59) and the Declaration
on Christian Education (n. 10) the human sciences in
using their own proper principles and method can never
be in contradiction with the faith.

Roman Catholic theology, which in the nineteenth
century had opposed modern liberties, by the time of the
Second Vatican Council had become a staunch defender of
human freedom and dignity. This emphasis appears in all
the conciliar documents but especially in the Pastoral
Constitution on the Church in the Modern World and in
the Declaration on Religious Freedom, which begins by
recognizing the demand for freedom in human society
regarding chiefly the quest for the values proper to the
human spirit (n. 1). Chapter eight will discuss the
increasing importance given to freedom in Catholic social
ethics. The emphasis on freedom and dignity in general,
together with the responsibility and role of the laity in the
church, stimulated the need to protect the rights of all in
the church. As a result, due process was often called for in
settling disputes within the church. Without spelling out
its meaning, the Pastoral Constitution on the Church in
the Modern World (n. 62) maintained that all the faithful
whether clerical or lay possess a lawful freedom of
inquiry, freedom of thought and of expressing their mind
with humility and fortitude in those matters on which
they enjoy competence.

In retrospect there is an intriguing analogy between the
acceptance of religious liberty in the Roman Catholic
Church and the acceptance of academic freedom by the
mainstream of Catholic educators in the United States.
Proponents of religious liberty in the nineteenth century
often based their position on a theory that there was no
place for faith, religion, or the church in society. Finally,
in the middle of the twentieth century a different rationale

was proposed for religious liberty based on the dignity of the human person and on the presupposition of a limited constitutional state which is not competent in matters of religion but which allows freedom for religion to flourish in society.

There can be no doubt that some of the proponents of academic freedom in the beginning were opposed to faith and dogma of any kind. At the very least it was often asserted that true knowledge could come only from the scientific method and not from faith. Faith was an unjustified intrusion on scientific inquiry with its heavy empirical orientation. Robert MacIver in his often-cited book stoutly argues against a positivistic notion of science but on the other hand betrays the one-sidedness of his approach when he asserts that what the scholar investigates is not values but evidences.[16] Also American Catholics were aware that academic freedom and the autonomy of institutions of higher learning had gone hand in hand with the fact that many colleges and universities which were originally started by Protestant denominations were no longer, or only minimally, related to the church. In addition, Catholics feared the secularism they saw in non-Catholic higher education.

By the late 1960s many Catholics recognized that the acceptance of academic freedom did not necessarily involve these other unfortunate consequences which in many ways were unacceptable to Catholics. First, faith and academic freedom were not necessarily opposed. The limitations of the scientific method and the value-free approach of much of earlier American higher education were coming under increasing criticism. The search for values, meaning, and the human is a most important academic function. Scientists themselves began to acknowledge that even the empirical sciences have their own presuppositions. Theology with its presupposition of faith is not the only academic discipline that functions on presuppositions that cannot be proved by the scientific method. Second, in Catholic circles discussions about academic freedom occurred in a context within which educators were discussing the Catholic identity of their

institutions. The majority of Catholic educators were
convinced that a Catholic identity can remain and be
efficacious in a free and autonomous institution of higher
learning. Academic freedom was championed without
having to endorse some of the negative aspects often
associated with it in the past.

III. Academic Freedom and Roman Catholic Theology

Statements by Catholic educators affirmed the need and
the place for full academic freedom in Catholic colleges
and universities, but such statements did not develop a
theological rationale for the most difficult aspect of the
question—the academic freedom of Roman Catholic
theology in the university setting. Not only Roman
Catholic thinkers but most secular academics had been
convinced that Roman Catholic theology on the campus
could not enjoy a complete academic freedom. This
section of the paper will argue that the academic freedom
of the Catholic theologian in the university not only is
legitimate but in the long run is most beneficial for the
Catholic institution, for theology, and for the church.

The defense of the academic freedom of the Catholic
theologian was worked out amid a number of practical
controversies at Catholic colleges and universities in the
United States in the 1960s, especially at The Catholic
University of America and at the University of Dayton.[17]
The problem can be succinctly stated. Roman Catholic
faith assigns a God-given role to the hierarchical magisterium of pope and bishops as the official and at times
even infallible teachers on questions of faith and morals.
The Roman Catholic theologian precisely as such must
recognize the role of the hierarchical magisterium and
therefore is not and cannot be free to come to a conclusion
in opposition to Catholic faith or to the divinely constituted hierarchical teaching office in the church.

Some attempts that were made to justify the academic
freedom of the Roman Catholic theologian seem to me to
be inadequate. According to John E. Walsh the Catholic

university should not be seen as an instrument of the church's teaching mission. Such an approach righty tries to distinguish and separate the roles of academic theology and of the hierarchical teaching church, but Walsh solves the problem by seeing the university as the church learning in distinction from the hierarchical magisterium as the church teaching.[18] The teaching function of the church cannot be reduced only to the teaching function of the hierarchical magisterium. In a true sense all the baptized also share in the teaching function of Jesus.

A second inadequate justification overemphasizes the secularization of the university so that the theology taught in a Catholic university is not merely Roman Catholic theology. In my judgment such an approach goes too far and destroys not only the academic discipline of Roman Catholic theology but also any real notion of a Catholic university. My justification rests on contemporary but quite widely accepted notions of the science of theology and of the relationship between the hierarchical magisterium and the role of theology. Both of these are disputed questions, but the position outlined below is in conformity with a very sizeable part of contemporary Roman Catholic theologizing.[19]

Theology is a scientific discipline, a human activity which presupposes faith. Faith itself is not primarily the revelation of propositions or even of truths. Faith is primarily the saving encounter with the living God. But there is a truth dimension to faith. The object of faith is the totally other mystery of God, so that our knowledge of God will never be perfect in this world. In addition to the lack of completion in our knowledge and concepts of God and faith, there is also the imperfection of the language and symbols used to express this faith. The acceptance of hermeneutics reminds us of the historically and culturally conditioned nature of our knowledge and of our verbal and symbolic expression of this knowledge. Theology has the never-ending task of trying to interpret better and understand more adequately the mystery of faith in the light of contemporary realities. No longer is theology understood in the light of a science seeking certitude based on a deductive methodology. Interpretation of the sources of revelation and of the teaching of the hierarchical magisterium in the light of the signs of the times is theology's function.

All must admit the God-given role of the hierarchical magisterium, but its relationship with the role of the theologians has been proposed in a different way by many contemporary theologians. To this day many bishops and Roman authorities follow an approach proposed by the theologians of the Roman school in the nineteenth century, according to which the role of theology is seen in terms of complete subordination to the hierarchical magisterium. Theology sets forth and defends the teaching of the hierarchical magisterium.

We in chapter one, together with many contemporary theologians, see a more complex relationship. Theology itself also has a pastoral dimension and is not merely a scientific discipline. The hierarchical magisterium has the function of teacher in faith and morals, but that teaching cannot avoid theology. History reminds us that the hierarchical church has been dependent upon theology for its own formulations. The interpretative function of theology must deal with and give correct weight to the teachings of the hierarchical magisterium so that through theological speculation our understanding might grow and deepen. Part of the theological function of interpretation of the hierarchical teaching involves the possibility of dissent from authoritative, noninfallible church teaching.[20] Theology must be free to responsibly exercise this interpretative function.

This understanding of the relationship of theology to the hierarchical magisterium acknowledges important aspects of subordination but also includes an interpretative function which should deepen and increase our understanding, but one that might possibly involve dissent from authoritative teaching. Here is the ultimate reason for the need of responsible freedom for Catholic theologians. Many proponents of this approach point out that historically there were mistakes and errors in some aspects of authoritative teachings which have been corrected, thanks at least partly to the work of theologians; e.g., the cases of Popes Liberius, Vigilius, Honorius, Alexander III, and thirteenth-century condemnations of Aristotle. Official church teaching has changed on a number of issues, at least partly with the assistance of theology—war and peace in the early church, reasons justifying sexual relations between spouses, interest taking, the right of the accused to keep silent, religious liberty. In the context of the Second Vatican Council it was easy to see the detrimental effects on the life of the church caused by the silencing of many theologians not only during the anti-Modernist period but until the council itself. In the United States John Tracy Ellis has chronicled the most significant cases in which the autonomy of the academic enterprise of Roman Catholic theology has not been respected by the hierarchical authorities in the Church.[21]

The procedure and institutions connected with academic freedom in American academe seem very apt for safeguarding the legitimate freedom of Roman Catholic theology and at the same time for recognizing the God-given teaching function of the hierarchical magisterium in faith and morals. How should this work in practice? The Roman Catholic theologian who enjoys academic freedom in the college or university has the correlative duties of responsibility and competency. Competency requires that one be true to the presuppositions, sources, and methods of the discipline. Specifically, the theologian should distinguish between the data of revelation and theories or hypotheses that have been proposed. The official teaching of the church should be carefully spelled out and interpreted in accord with accepted hermeneutic principles. Personal hypotheses and opinions should be labeled as such. The personal responsibility of the competent theologian forms the best safeguard for protecting the rights of all concerned.

If the Roman Catholic theologian is not competent, then the professor can be dismissed for cause just as an incompetent physicist or anthropologist can be dismissed for cause in accord with the principles of academic due process. However, the judgment about incompetency must be made by academic peers. In the case of the theologian the peers must give due weight to all official church teaching in arriving at their judgment. Church authority as such has no direct power to intervene juridically in academe, for then the autonomy of academe is violated. Church teaching authority can point out for the good of the church that the theory of a particular theologian is erroneous, but the judgment about dismissal must be made by academic peers giving due weight to official church teaching. Such procedures, although not perfect, safeguard both the God-given hierarchical teaching function and the role of theology.

In practice many have accepted the procedure protecting the academic freedom of the Roman Catholic theologian in academe as explained above. In this light there is no need to require any limitation on the academic freedom of the Roman Catholic theologian. "The Catholic University in the Modern World," a statement issued by the Second International Congress of Delegates of Catholic Universities, outlines such a process for institutions not juridically erected by Rome.[22] The Faculty Inquiry Board at the Catholic University of America proposed such an approach in its decision about the theologians who dissented from aspects of the papal teaching in *Humanae vitae* condemning artificial contraception.[23] This section has attempted to establish the need of academic freedom for the Roman Catholic theologian in academe not merely on pragmatic grounds but on a theological consideration of the role of theology and its relation to the hierarchical magisterium. Such academic freedom would exist not only for the good of the Catholic university but also for the good of theology and of the whole church.

IV. New Church Regulations, Theology, and Academic Freedom

On April 15, 1979, Pope John Paul II issued *Sapientia christiana,* an apostolic constitution containing the new law and regulations for ecclesiastical universities which are canonically erected and approved.[24] On the basis of these regulations universities and faculties are to submit their statutes to the Sacred Congregation for Education for approval. All those who teach disciplines concerning faith or morals must receive a canonical mission from the chancellor of the university, "for they do not teach on their own authority but by virtue of the mission they have received from the Church" (art. 27). To acquire a tenured position or the highest faculty rank the candidate needs a declaration of *nihil obstat* from the Holy See (art. 27). Also the document stresses that teachers are to carry on their work in full communion with the authentic magisterium of the church (art. 26; 70).

If interpreted literally and without any accommodation to local academic conditions, the constitution stands in opposition to the understanding proposed in this paper. According to the most obvious interpretation of the new apostolic constitution, the Catholic college and university is not autonomous but is a continuation of the teaching function of the hierarchical magisterium. Such a relationship explains why teachers need the *nihil obstat* from Rome and teachers in disciplines concerning faith and morals also need a canonical mission. In such a situation there is no academic freedom because judgments about competency are not made by peers, and promotion and tenure depend on judgments made by church authority as such.

In the light of this new document one can point out clear differences emerging between the constitution and many Catholic educators. In the 1960s the international Federation of Catholic Universities (IFCU) began considering the question of the nature and structure of a Catholic university. The Land O'Lakes statement quoted above was prepared by the North American region of the federation in preparation for the meeting at Kinshasa in 1968, but that meeting did not accept the notion of autonomy and academic freedom proposed in the North American document. At the First International Congress of Delegates of Catholic Universities held in Rome in 1969 the positions proposed in the Land O'Lakes statement were generally acknowledged, but the Congregation for Education did not accept this document. Finally, the second congress issued its statement "The Catholic University in the Modern World," which accepted the basic wording of the Land O'Lakes statement calling for true autonomy and academic freedom in the Catholic university (n. 20). For institutions which are not canonically erected by Rome the Congress document calls for procedures similar to those developed in the previous section of this article (n. 59). The Congregation for Education had some misgivings about these aspects of the document but allowed the document to be circulated as the work of the congress.[25]

If the apostolic constitution is literally applied, it will mean that such canonically erected Catholic institutions cannot be true universities in the accepted sense of the term in the United States. Likewise, the theology done in such institutions will not have the necessary academic freedom to perform its function properly. As a result, canonically erected universities, Roman Catholic theology, and the good of the whole church will suffer.

The apostolic constitution *Sapientia christiana* applies only to pontifical universities and faculties and hence would not affect most Catholic institutions of higher learning in the United States. However, the proposed new code of canon law, which will probably go into effect in the near future, in Book III, Canon 64 states that all who teach theology or disciplines related to theology in any Catholic institution of higher learning need a canonical mission. Again, if applied literally and without any accommodation to American academic principles, this legislation threatens the autonomy of all Catholic colleges and universities.

NOTES

1. Arthur O. Lovejoy, "Academic Freedom," *Encyclopedia of the Social Sciences,* ed. Edwin R.A. Seligman and Alvin Johnson (New York: Macmillan Co., 1930), I, 384.

2. Richard Hofstadter and Walter P. Metzger, *Academic Freedom in the United States* (New York: Columbia University Press, 1955).

3. For the significant documents, statements, and actions of the AAUP together with important essays on academic freedom, see *Academic Freedom and Tenure: A Handbook of the American Association of University Professors,* ed. Louis Joughin (Madison, Wisconsin: University of Wisconsin Press, 1969). Subsequent statements and actions of the AAUP are found in *AAUP Bulletin,* which since 1979 is called *Academe: Bulletin of the AAUP.*

4. Louis Joughin, "Academic Due Process," in *Academic Freedom and Tenure,* pp. 264-305.

5. *Academic Freedom and Tenure,* pp. 159; 36.

6. Sidney Hook, *Heresy, Yes—Conspiracy, No* (New York: John Day Co., 1953), p. 220.

7. Robert M. MacIver, *Academic Freedom in Our Time* (New York: Columbia University Press, 1955), pp. 134-146.

8. Cited by MacIver, ibid., p. 135.

9. Charles Donahue, "Freedom and Education: The Pluralist Background," *Thought* 27 (1952-1953), 542-560; "Freedom and Education: The Sacral Problem," *Thought* 28 (1953-1954), 209-233; "Freedom and Education, III: Catholicism and Academic Freedom," *Thought* 29 (1954-1955), 555-573; also, "Heresy and Conspiracy," *Thought* 28 (1953-1954), 528-546; Aldo J. Tos, "A Critical Study of American Views on Academic Freedom" (Ph.D. dissertation, The Catholic University of America, 1958).

10. Gerard F. Kreyche, "American Catholic Higher Learning and Academic Freedom" *National Catholic Education Association Bulletin* 62 (August 1965), 211-222. For historical information on academic freedom and Catholic institutions in the United States, see various writings of Philip Gleason including: "Academic Freedom and the Crisis in Catholic Universities," in

Academic Freedom and the Catholic University, ed. Edward
Manier and John W. Houck (Notre Dame, Ind.: Fides Publishers, 1967), 33-56; "Academic Freedom: Survey, Retrospect and
Prospects," *National Catholic Education Association Bulletin*
64 (August 1967), 67-74; "Freedom and the Catholic University," *National Catholic Education Association Bulletin* 65
(November 1968), 21-29.

11. For a book of significant articles based on that symposium
and for a summary of the discussions that occurred, see
Academic Freedom and the Catholic University, ed. Edward
Manier and John W. Houck.

12. Frederick Walter Gunti, "Academic Freedom as an
Operative Principle for the Catholic Theologian," (S.T.D.
dissertation, The Catholic University of America, 1969). For the
1958 dissertation, see Tos in footnote 9.

13. This document has been reprinted in many places. For the
text of this and other documents on Catholic universities,
together with significant essays on various aspects of academic
freedom and the catholic university in the contemporary world,
see *The Catholic University: A Modern Appraisal*, ed. Neil G.
McCluskey (Notre Dame, Ind.: University of Notre Dame Press,
1970), p. 336.

14. "Freedom, Autonomy and the University," *IDOC International: North American Edition* 39 (January 15, 1972), 86;83.

15. John Tracy Ellis sparked the debate with his provocative
article "American Catholics and the Intellectual Life," *Thought*
30 (1955), 351-388. See also Walter J. Ong, *Frontiers in
American Catholicism* (New York: Macmillan Co., 1957);
Thoman F. O'Dea, *American Catholic Dilemma: An Inquiry
into the Intellectual Life* (New York: Sheed and Ward, 1958).

16. MacIver, *Academic Freedom in Our Time*, p. 141.

17. For an overview of these and other problems, see John
Kelley, "Academic Freedom and the Catholic College Theologian," in *Theology in Revolution*, ed. George Devine (Staten
Island, New York: Alba House, 1970), pp. 169-183; John Tracy
Ellis, "A Tradition of Autonomy?" in *The Catholic University:
A Modern Appraisal*, especially pp. 252-270. In 1967 the trustees
of Catholic University did not renew the contract of a professor
who had been unanimously approved by all the academic
committees of the university for promotion. After a faculty and

student strike lasting almost a week the professor was given his contract and promotion. In 1968 twenty Catholic University professors signed a public statement of dissent from the specific teaching of *Humanae Vitae* condemning artificial contraception. Despite some significant abuses in procedures the Catholic University trustees followed academic due process and ordered a hearing by a faculty board of inquiry which vindicated the statement and actions of the professors. See Charles E. Curran, Robert E. Hunt, et al., *Dissent in and for the Church: Theologians and Humanae Vitae* (New York: Sheed and Ward, 1969) and John F. Hunt and Terrence R. Connelly, *The Responsibility of Dissent: The Church and Academic Freedom* (New York: Sheed and Ward, 1969). At Dayton one of the lay instructors charged several of his colleagues with heresy.

18. John E. Walsh, "The University and the Church," in *Academic Freedom and the Catholic University*, pp. 103-118.

19. My position here summarizes what has been developed at much greater length in the volumes mentioned in footnote 17. For similar approaches, see Gunti and Robert E. Hunt, "Academic Freedom and the Theologian," *Proceedings of the Catholic Theological Society of America* 23 (1968), 261-267.

20. For a recent summary of present-day discussions on the nature of hierarchical magisterium, see *Chicago Studies* 17 (Summer 1978). This special issue is entitled "The Magisterium, the Theologian and the Educator."

21. John Tracy Ellis, "A Tradition of Autonomy?" in *The Catholic University: A Modern Appraisal*, pp. 206-270.

22. This statement is published in a number of places including *Catholic Mind* 71 (May 1973), 25-44. This particular point is made at n. 59, pp. 42-43.

23. "Report of Catholic University Board of inquiry regarding Expressions of Theological Dissent by Faculty members on Encyclical *Humanae Vitae*," *AAUP Bulletin* 55 (1969), 264-266. Interpretive comments by relevant committees on the 1940 statement of AAUP show that most church-related institutions no longer need or desire the departure from the principle of academic freedom implied in the 1940 statement and the AAUP does not endorse such a departure, *AAUP Bulletin* 56 (1970), 166, 167.

24. For an English translation, see *Origins: N.C. Documen-*

tary Service 9, n. 3 (June 7, 1979), 34-45.

25. For the history of these developments within regional and international groups of Catholic educators, see Neil G. Mc-Cluskey, "Introduction: This Is How It Happened," in *The Catholic University: A Modern Appraisal*, pp. 1-28, and Robert J. Henle, "Catholic Universities and the Vatican," *America* 136 (April 9, 1977), 315-322. It should be reported that a December 1976 meeting in Rome attended only by delegates of canonically erected universities and faculties (almost all American Catholic colleges and universities are not canonically erected except for some faculties at The Catholic University of America) voted in favor of a *nihil obstat* for tenured professors and for professors in the highest rank. See "Delegates Approve Vatican Consent for Professors," *Our Sunday Visitor* 65 (December 19, 1976), 1.

PART TWO

Methodological Questions

3. A Methodological Overview of Fundamental Moral Theology

Moral theology, like all theology, bases its reflections on the Word of God in the scriptures, on tradition, on the teaching of the church, on the signs of the times, and on the eschatological pull of the future. In the last few years great attention has been paid to the signs of the times. The signs of the times, which are important for moral theology in the United States, include both the cultural milieu with its understanding of moral problems and the thematic and systematic reflection, which is the discipline of ethics, both in its religious and philosophical contexts.

To read the signs of the times always involves a prudential discernment and the risk of being wrong. Traditionally American life and ethos have given great importance to freedom in all aspects of life, but there has also been a recognition of the limits of freedom which has especially come to the fore in recent years. The contemporary American scene has witnessed the end of an era in which easy optimism and even naïveté characterized much of the country's self-understanding. Self-criticism and doubt have been more apparent ever since the Vietnam War, Watergate, continuing world crises, and the energy shortage. At times there is a feeling of pessimism and even helplessness, but this self-critical attitude has raised in the public consciousness a greater interest in ethics and the morality of the decisions that must be made to guide our future life. No one is unaware of the multitude of problems calling out for a solution:

nuclear energy and weapons; poverty throughout the world and at home; hunger in the world; human rights and wars of liberation; the contemporary trouble spots in the globe—the Near East, Indochina, Africa, Central and South America; world trade and economic policies; multinational corporations; technology; energy; the environment. There appears to be a widespread feeling that Americans must be willing to face these problems and also to change their own life styles away from the consumerism and materialism which have so often characterized our society. At the same time there exists a great interest in contemplation, in the personal struggle for growth, and in the meaning of life and death.

The influence of specifically Catholic thought and theology on the American cultural and intellectual life has not been great. Over twenty years ago John Tracy Ellis criticized American Catholicism for its failures in making any noticeable contribution to the wider scene of American intellectual and cultural life.[1] Since that time individual Catholics and groups have made some contributions, but generally speaking there has been little that is specifically theological in these individual contributions.

On the reflective level of ethics as such, Catholic moral theology in the United States is related to and influenced by religious ethics, especially Protestant Christian ethics, and philosophical ethics. Protestant ethics has had a significant influence in the United States. Perhaps there is no intellectual figure who had a greater impact on American foreign policy in the middle years of the twentieth century than theologian Reinhold Niebuhr.[2] Before the Second Vatican Council there was little or no dialogue between Protestant and Catholic ethicists, but that situation has changed dramatically since the 1960s. Not only dialogue but also rapprochement characterizes the relationship between Catholic moral theology and Protestant ethics. As one very knowledgeable and competent Protestant scholar has pointed out, Catholic moral theology now gives more stress to aspects of ethics that were previously identified as typically Protestant emphases—becoming, process, dynamism, change, freedom, history, grace, and gospel. On the other hand, Protestants have striven to give more importance to Catholic concerns such as being, structure, order, continuity, nature, and law.[3] Close contact and dialogue with Protestant Christian ethics characterizes moral theology in the United States, but moral theology still attempts to remain firmly rooted in its own tradition. At the same time there is increasing communication with philosophical ethics both on methodological and on substantive questions. Philosophical ethics is no longer dominated by an analytic approach which shuns substantive and content questions. Now there is a growing interest of philosophers in the ethical questions facing society and in theoretical issues such as justice and the justification of moral norms.[4] Catholic moral theology exists in an intellectual milieu in the United States in which it is in contact and dialogue with Protestant and philosophical ethics. In the light of these signs of the times this chapter will discuss method in moral theology.

I approach the question of method in moral theology with the presupposition that errors and mistakes in method generally arise not so much from positive error as from the failure to consider all the aspects which deserve discussion. In moral theology itself in the last few years there has been an unfortunate tendency, readily understandable in the light of the contemporary controversies, to reduce moral theology merely to the question of norms and the morality of specific actions. The questions of specific actions and of norms are significant questions in moral theology, but there are other questions which are of greater or equal importance. In my judgment the following areas must be investigated in any systematic reflection on Christian moral life: the perspective or stance; the ethical model; Christian anthropology; concrete Christian decision-making and norms. These different aspects will now be discussed in greater detail.

I. Stance

The question of stance or perspective is the most fundamental and logically first consideration in moral theology. Catholic moral theology has not explicitly posed the question of stance, but in the American Protestant tradition James Sellers has insisted on stance as the first consideration in moral theology, logically prior to any other consideration and the source of other criteria.[5] James Gustafson employs a similar concept of perspective or posture to indicate the fundamental angle of vision which directs the entire enterprise of Christian ethics.[6]

Two cautions should be kept in mind in any discussion of stance. First, it is impossible to say that one stance is right and another wrong. The adequacy of the stance depends on how well it accomplishes its purpose as being the logically prior step which structures our understanding of moral reality, serves as a critique of other approaches, and is a source of other ethical criteria. Second, although stance as a logically prior step seems to have something of the apriori about it, in reality my own stance developed in an aposteriori way based on a critique of other positions. To properly fulfill its critical function and be proved adequate, the stance cannot rest merely on an apriori deduction or assumption.

My stance consists of a perspective based on the fivefold Christian mysteries of creation, sin, incarnation, redemption, and resurrection destiny. The reason for accepting these as aspects of the stance are obvious for the Christian, but the adequacy of this fivefold stance must be shown. The stance functions both methodologically and substantively. From a methodological viewpoint the stance both serves as a negative critique of other methodologies and provides a positive approach of its own.

Roman Catholic natural law theory rightly recognizes that the Christian finds ethical wisdom and knowledge not only in the scriptures and in Jesus Christ but also in human nature and human reason. On the basis of creation by a good and gracious God, human reason reflecting on human nature can arrive at ethical wisdom and knowledge. Insistence on the goodness of the natural and the human, with its corollary that grace builds on nature and is not opposed to nature, stands as a hallmark of the Catholic theological tradition. Some Protestant theologians deny the goodness of creation and the possibility of ethical wisdom and knowledge based on human nature and human reason for a number of different reasons—scripture alone is the source of ethical wisdom for the Christian; a narrow Christomonism sees Christ as the only way into the ethical problem; sin so affects human nature and human reason that they cannot serve as the basis of true knowledge; an unwillingness to accept an analogy between creation and the creator.

However, from the viewpoint of the proposed stance, the natural-law approach is deficient because it does not integrate the natural or creation into the total Christian perspective. The natural-law theory rightly recognizes creation and incarnation, but sin, redemption, and resurrection destiny do not receive their due. Catholic moral theology may have overstressed sin in terms of particular actions, but it never paid sufficient attention to the reality of sin as present in the world and affecting, without however destroying, human nature and human reason. Likewise, natural-law theory gives no place to grace, or redemption and resurrection destiny as the stance describes this reality, so that often Catholic moral theology became based exclusively on the natural to the neglect of what was then called the supernatural.

On the contrary, a Lutheran two-realm theory recognizes the reality of sin but overemphasizes sin and fails to give enough importance to the reality of creation and to moral wisdom based on it, to the integrating effect of the incarnation, to the recognition that redemption also affects the world in which we live, and to a more positive appreciation of the relationship between resurrection destiny and the present world.

Protestant liberalism arose in the nineteenth century, and its most significant ethical manifestation in the United States was the Social Gospel school.[7] This approach, especially in its more extreme forms, stressed the goodness of creation, the integrating effect of the incarnation on all reality, and the presence of redemption in the world, but sin and resurrection destiny as a future gift at the end of time were neglected.

Liberalism was succeeded in Protestant theology by neoorthodoxy with its Barthian and Niebuhrian approaches. Barthian ethics flourished in Europe, but its most significant American exponent is Paul Lehmann.[8] Barthian ethics emphasized the centrality of redemption and of Christ and made Christ the sole way into the ethical problem. There was no place for philosophical ethics or natural law for the Christian. Within such a perspective, sin, incarnation, redemption, and resurrection destiny could all be given due importance, but creation and its ethical ramifications in terms of human reason were denied. Niebuhrian Christian realism, which ultimately exerted such a great influence on American thought and foreign policy, recognized some ethical import in creation even though it was infected by sin, but in the final analysis gave too much to the presence of sin and failed to appreciate the effects of incarnation, redemption, and a more positive relationship between the world of the present and the fullness of resurrection destiny in the eschaton. However, in many ways Niebuhr tried to account for all the elements in the stance but overemphasized the role of sin and downplayed the others.

In the 1960s in Protestant theology some approaches similar to the older liberalism came to the fore in the form of the theologies of the death of God and of secularization. Once again there was a tendency to overstress creation, incarnation, and redemption and to neglect the reality of sin and the fact that resurrection destiny is future and its fullness comes only as God's gracious gift at the end of time. In the light of the proposed stance subsequent developments were healthy. A theology of secularization gave way to a theology of hope with the primacy on resurrection destiny as future. However, at times there was still not enough emphasis on sin and on some discontinuity between this world and the next. Moltmann as a Protestant and Metz as a Catholic both went through a development similar to that outlined above and then put greater emphasis on discontinuity by highlighting the role of suffering as Moltmann wrote about *The Crucified God* and Metz talked about the future *"ex memoria passionis eius."*[9]

In the 1960s in conjunction with the Second Vatican Council, Roman Catholic theology rightly attempted to overcome the dichotomy between nature and grace, between gospel and daily life, between church and world. But in overcoming the dichotomy there emerged the danger of making everything grace and the supernatural. In other words, there was a tendency to forget sin and the fact that resurrection destiny is future and exists always in discontinuity, as well as in continuity, with present reality. Catholic thinking in this period often suffered from a collapsed eschaton because of which people thought that the fullness of the kingdom would come quickly, readily, and without struggle or suffering.

In contemporary Catholic theology, liberation theology, with its attempt to integrate redemption and the gospel into our understanding of political and economic life in society, marks an improvement over the exclusive natural-law approach that formerly characterized Catholic social ethics as exemplified in the papal social encyclicals. However, in liberation theology there exists among some a tendency to forget the reality of sin as affecting to some extent all reality (too often the impression is given that sin is all on one side) and a tendency to think that the fullness of the eschaton will come too readily and quickly. On the contrary, liberation will involve a long, hard, difficult struggle and will never be fully present in this world. At times liberation theology fails to recognize complexity in this world, for among some there is a great confidence in being able to know quite easily what God is doing in this world. The opposite danger maintains that reality is complex, and sin so affects all reality that one cannot know what God is doing in the world. I want to avoid both these extremes.

Not only does the stance embracing the fivefold mysteries of creation, sin, incarnation, redemption, and resurrection destiny serve as a critique of many other theories in moral theology as pointed out above, but at the same time it provides a positive methodology and perspective for approaching moral theology. Creation indicates the goodness of the human and human reason; but sin touches all reality, without, however, destroying the basic goodness of creation. Incarnation integrates all reality into the plan of God's kingdom. Redemption as already present affects all reality, while resurrection destiny as future exists in continuity with the redeemed present but also in discontinuity because the fullness of the kingdom remains God's gracious gift at the end of time.

The stance also addresses some substantive issues; but since the stance is the logically prior step in moral theology and by definition remains somewhat general, one cannot expect the stance to provide specific and detailed substantive content. A primary contribution of the stance is in giving a direction and general perspective to our understanding of some of the most basic issues in Christian ethics. The first question concerns the meaning of human existence in this world and the relationship between this world and the kingdom. In the past Protestant theology often addressed the same basic question in terms of the relationship between Christ and culture as illustrated in the work of H. Richard Niebuhr, who points out five different typologies for understanding this relationship.[10] The position derived from the stance corresponds to Niebuhr's type of Christ-transforming culture. The fullness of the kingdom will only come at the end, but in this world the kingdom strives to make itself more present. The individual Christian and the community of believers must recognize that the mission of the church and of the gospel calls for them to struggle for peace and justice in the world.

The stance also sheds light on the meaning of death for the Christian. Death seems to point to total discontinuity between this world and the next for the individual person, but in the light of the stance death can be seen in a transformationist perspective. All created reality will die, but sin has added an important negative dimension to the Christian understanding of death. Even more importantly, death is understood in the light of the mystery of the incarnation, death, and resurrection of Jesus, so that death is neither the end nor the beginning of something totally discontinuous but rather the transformation of earthly life and reality into the fullness of life and love.

The stance serves as an interpretive tool in understanding the basic mysteries of the Christian life. Especially in a sacramental and mystical perspective the Christian life is often described in terms of living out the paschal mystery of Jesus into which we are baptized. The paschal mystery can be interpreted in different ways depending on the stance. Some have interpreted it in paradoxical terms to show that life is present in the midst of death, joy in the midst of sorrow, and light in darkness. A transformationist understanding recognizes that there are some paradoxical aspects to the Christian life, but also at times God's life is known in human life, God's love in human love, God's light in human light, and God's joy in human joy. The paschal mystery understood in this perspective gives us a better understanding of Christian life and death and the relationship between the two. Life involves a constant dying to selfishness and sin to enter more fully into the resurrection, and so death itself can be seen as the moment of growth par excellence—dying to the present to enter most fully into life itself.

Perhaps this is the best place to mention briefly the debate about a distinctively Christian ethic, which will be discussed in greater detail in the next chapter. I deny that on the level of material content (actions, virtues, attitudes, and dispositions) there is anything distinctively Christian because non-Christians can and do share the same material content of morality even to the point of such attitudes as self-sacrificing love. Unlike some others, I base this, not on a common human nature abstractly considered, but rather on the fact that in the present existential order all are called to share in the fullness of God's love. However, Christians thematize their understanding in a specifically Christian way. Since ethics, as distinguished from morality, is a thematic and systematic reflection, moral theology and Christian ethics must be based on Christian realities even though some of these (e.g., creation) are not distinctively Christian.

II. Ethical Model

The second logical step in the systematic reflection, which is moral theology, concerns the model in view of which one understands the Christian life. Three different models have been proposed in both philosophical and theological literature. The teleological model views the ethical life in terms of the goal or end to be achieved, but in the complexity of existence one distinguishes ultimate goals from intermediate and subordinate goals. Something is morally good if it is conducive to achieving the goal and is evil if it prevents the attainment of the goal. It should be pointed out that these models are very broad umbrellas. Thomas Aquinas, who begins his ethical consideration with a discussion of the last end, serves as a good example of the teleological model, but utilitarians also fit under the same model. A deontological model views the moral life primarily in terms of duty, law, or obligation. The categorical imperative of Immanuel Kant well illustrates a deontological approach to ethics. Popular Christian piety frequently adopts such an approach by making the ten commandments the basis of the moral life. The manuals of moral theology, although thinking they were in the tradition of Thomas Aquinas, by their heavy emphasis on law as the objective norm of morality and conscience as the subjective norm, belong to the deontological model. A relationality-responsibility model views the moral life primarily in terms of the person's multiple relationships with God, neighbor, world, and self and the subject's actions in this context.

I opt for a relationality-responsibility model as the primary ethical model. Such an option does not exclude some place for teleological and deontological concerns, but the relationality-responsibility model is primary and forms the perimeters within which the ethical life is discussed. There are a number of significant reasons supporting the primacy of such a model. Contemporary scriptural studies indicate that the primary ethical concept in the Old Testament is not law but covenant. The New Testament emphasis on love as at least an important ethical concern, despite its different understandings by different authors, argues for a relationality-responsibility approach. The scriptures often describe the moral life as our response to the gracious gift of God. Contemporary hermeneutics reminds us of the difficulty of finding universal moral norms in the scriptures.[11] Among Protestants a Barthian approach argued against a fundamentalistic reading of the scriptures often associated with legalism and replaced it with an understanding of the scriptures as the description of the mighty acts of God to which the believer responds. The stance reminds us of the call for the Christian to respond creatively to the contemporary situation and to make the kingdom more present. Philosophical emphases on historical consciousness, the importance of the subject, and personalism argue against the more static notion of morality as the plan of God worked out for all eternity which so often characterized Catholic understandings in the past. Although the teleological model might be more open to historicity, personalism, and the importance of the subject, still one does not have as much control over one's life as this model often supposes.

Within a relationality-responsibility model one must avoid the danger of a narrow personalism which views the moral life only in terms of the perspective of an "I-thou" relationship. The Christian is related to God, neighbor, the world, and self. The failure to give due weight to all these relationships will distort the meaning of the Christian life. The basic reality of the Christian life has been described in different ways—love, conversion, life in Christ, the law of the Spirit. All of these descriptions can be used, but they must be understood in terms of a relationality model which includes all the aspects mentioned above.

Just as the fundamental, positive understanding of the Christian life is viewed in relational terms, so too the

negative aspect of sin should be seen in the same perspective. A deontological model defines sin as an act against
the law of God. A teleological model views sin as going
against God, the ultimate end. But from the earliest pages
of Genesis sin is described in terms of our relationship
with God, neighbor, the world, and self. A contemporary
theology of sin in terms of the fundamental option should
also be interpreted in relational terms. Mortal sin is
primarily, not an act against the law of God or going
against the ultimate end, but rather the breaking of our
relationship of love with God, neighbor, world, and self.
Venial sin is the diminishing of these fundamental
relationships. In this perspective all the aspects of sin
become apparent, especially social sin and its influence on
our political, social, and economic structures.

Changes in the understanding of the sacrament of
penance well illustrate the shift to a more relational model
of the Christian life. In the context of a deontological
ethical model the sacrament of penance was called confession from the name of the primary act—the confession of
sins according to number and species. Today the sacrament is called reconciliation—a relational term which
includes our multiple relationships with God, neighbor,
world, and self.

The general notion of relationality-responsibility needs
to be developed and spelled out as accurately as possible.
On the American scene H. Richard Niebuhr has attempted a further elucidation of this basic concept.
Niebuhr understands responsibility as involving four
elements—response, interpretation, accountability, and
social solidarity.[12] My own development of relationality-
responsibility, especially in comparison with Niebuhr,
gives more significance to the ontological grounding of
relationality and to the creative role of the subject.
Without using the term relationality-responsibility, Daniel C. Maguire has recently proposed a method which fits
under such a model. According to Maguire one seeks to
discover the moral reality on the basis of four sets of
questions—What?; Why? How? Who? When? Where?;
Forseeable effects?; Viable alternatives? The evaluation of

this moral reality involves a number of factors including creative imagination, reason and analysis, principles, affectivity, individual experience, group experience, authority, comedy, and tragedy.[13]

A relationality-responsibility model also influences our approach to particular questions. Take the example of lying. An older approach, based on the teleology inscribed by nature in the faculty of speech, defined the malice of lying as frustrating the God-given purpose of the faculty of speech, which according to God's plan is to express on one's lips what is in one's mind. Within such a context it was necessary to resort to a casuistry of mental reservations to deal with some of the problems that arise. Lately a different approach employing a relationality model has seen the malice of lying in the violation of my neighbor's right to truth. There are cases in which the neighbor does not have the right to truth, and my false speech does not involve the moral malice of lying. Similarly, in questions of sexuality, contraception and sterilization were condemned on the basis of the innate teleology inscribed in the sexual faculty. To go directly against the procreative purpose of the sexual faculty is always wrong. A more relational approach sees the sexual faculty related to the human person and the person related to others, especially to the marriage partner. For the good of the marriage relationship contraception or sterilization can be justified. A relationality-responsibility model not only determines our understanding of basic moral considerations but also results in different solutions to concrete ethical questions.

III. Christian Anthropology

A third step in the development of a method for moral theology concerns Christian anthropology, or the subject existing in the midst of these multiple relationships. In ethics the basic importance of the person is twofold. First, individual actions come from the person and are expressive of the person. Actions are ethically grounded in the person placing the actions. As the scriptures remind us, the good tree brings forth good fruit, or those who live in the Spirit should produce the fruits of the Spirit. Second, the person, through one's actions, develops and constitutes oneself as a moral subject. In the transcendental terms to be developed later, through one's actions one fulfills the drive to authentic self-transcendence. Individual acts are not the most fundamental ethical category because they are both expressive of the moral subject and constitutive of the moral being of the subject.

The importance of the moral subject underscores the place of growth and development in the Christian life. The Christian is called to be perfect even as the heavenly Father is perfect. Although the fullness of response to God's gracious gift will never be achieved, the Christian strives to grow in wisdom, age, and grace before God and human beings. The call to continual conversion also highlights the importance of growth in the Christian life. Philosophically this growth is grounded in the drive of the subject toward authentic self-transcendence. Through actions the subject continually transcends self and thereby contributes to true growth. Psychologists, too, have been paying much attention to the importance of moral growth in human life. Lawrence Kohlberg has proposed his theory of moral development involving six stages, with the last stage exemplifying postconventional morality and described as the full development of an interior, self-directed moral sense with an orientation of conscience toward ethical principles which appeal to logical comprehensiveness, universality, and consistency.[14] Catholic thinkers are appreciative of Kohlberg's work but are beginning to deal with Kohlberg in a critical way.[15] In my judgment Kohlberg's basic limits come from the formal aspect of his approach which is conditioned both by his Kantian philosophy and by his attempt to come up with a model of moral development acceptable and usable in a pluralistic context. As a result, his approach is based on the formalities of justice but does not give enough importance to content, to questions of dispositions and virtues, and to aspects other than a rationalistic understanding of justice.

Intimately connected with the person are the attitudes, virtues, and dispositions, which are expressed in action and which also constitute the subject as morally good and form an essential part of the growth and development of the moral subject.[16] These dispositions or virtues affect the various relationships within which the subject finds oneself. It is impossible to describe in detail all the dispositions which should characterize the different relationships within which the Christian person exists as subject, but some of the more significant ones can be mentioned.

Traditionally the relationship of the individual to God is characterized by the three theological virtues of faith, hope, and charity. In the light of a better integrated view of the moral life of the Christian based on the stance, some other important dispositions and attitudes should be developed. The attitude of worship and thanksgiving must characterize the Christian, who recognizes God as the author of love, life, and all good gifts. The Christian is primarily a worshipper. Here one can see the intimate connection between liturgy and the moral life of the Christian. The liturgy with its celebration of the encounter of God's giving and of human response mirrors the basic structure of life. A second very fundamental attitude for the Christian is openness and receptivity to the word and work of God. The scriptures frequently allude to the importance of this basic virtue—be it done unto me according to your will. This disposition is the true humility of spirit which the scriptures portray as the great characteristic of the poor of Yahweh. The privileged people in the kingdom—the poor, children, and sinners—underscore the importance of this disposition of openness to God's saving gift. A self-sufficiency, which so often characterizes the rich, the proud, and the important, is the antithesis of the disposition of openness or true humility of spirit.

Within the traditional triad of faith, hope, and charity more importance must be given to hope than was true in the manuals of moral theology. This emphasis comes from the contemporary theological highlighting of eschatology and of the pilgrim nature of our existence.

Struggle and suffering are an integral part of our existence.

Relationships to neighbor are characterized by the generic dispositions of love and justice. These general attitudes are then specified by the different relationships one has to specific neighbors—parent, friend, teacher, coworker, client, supervisor, employer, person in authority. In this context one cannot underscore enough the Christian insistence on love for the poor, the needy, and the outcast. This habitual attitude constantly calls one out of one's own narrowness and selfishness and strives to make ever broader and more universal the horizons of our love.

The relationship to the world and to earthly realities involves a number of specific relationships. The basic Christian attitude is that the goods of creation exist to serve the needs of all. The purpose of the goods of creation is to serve all God's people, and no one has a right to arrogate superfluous goods to oneself at the expense of the neighbor in need. Unfortunately an overemphasis on private property has too often blinded us to the basic attitude toward the goods of creation.[17] Selfishness and sinfulness have too often turned the goods of creation into the means of personal gratification and aggrandizement at the expense of others. The question of the best economic system is complex, but the guiding principle must be how well the system fulfills the basic principle that the goods of creation exist to serve the needs of all. An attitude of respectful gratitude for the gifts of creation serves as the basis for an environmental ethics. Our relationships with the different types of material goods will make more specific and spell out this general understanding of their universal destiny.

Our relationship to self is governed by the basic attitude of stewardship, using our gifts, talents, and selves in the living out of the Christian life. Here, too, the individual must always struggle against the opposite attitude of selfishness. As in our other relationships there is place for a proper Christian asceticism, which uses our lives, our gifts, and our bodies for the service of the kingdom and our own proper development.

IV. Decision Making and Norms

The fourth and final level of ethical reflection in describing a method for moral theology concerns concrete decision making and the morality of particular actions. In the contemporary context the two most important questions are the grounding of moral norms and the role and function of conscience.

There has been much discussion in Catholic moral theology, in Protestant Christian ethics, and in contemporary philosophical ethics about norms and the grounding of moral norms. Among a good number of Roman Catholic theologians throughout the world there has been a dissatisfaction with the existence of certain negative moral absolutes and the grounding of these norms in a particular understanding of natural law. In my judgment the problem arises from a concept of natural law as coinciding with the physical structure of the act, so that the physical structure of the act becomes morally normative—an act described in physical terms is said to be always and everywhere wrong. I am not saying that the physical structure of the act and the moral reality of the act cannot coincide, but the moral must include much more than merely the physical structure of the act and the grounding of the moral meaning involves more than merely a consideration of the physical structure of the act.

Many revisionist Catholic moral theologians at the present time solve the problem by distinguishing between moral evil and premoral, physical, or ontic evil, which, in the understanding of the manuals on questions such as double effect or sterilization, was called moral evil. Physical, ontic, or premoral evil can be justified if there is a commensurate or proportionate reason.[18]

In my view such an approach is in the right vein but does not go far enough. The physical is but one aspect of the moral, which is the ultimate human judgment and includes all the other aspects—the psychological, the sociological, the pedagogical, the hygenic, etc. It is necessary to reveal what is meant by premoral or ontic evil and commensurate reason. This raises the question of the different values involved. In general, norms exist to protect and promote values. But the question arises of how norms are arrived at and gounded?

Before discussing the precise way in which norms as the safeguard of values are to be grounded, a word should be said about the source of conflict situations, which bring about the tensions existing between and among different values. Again, in keeping with a general presumption in favor of complexity, there appear to be numerous sources for the conflict situations that arise and might call for modifications or exceptions in moral norms. From a strictly ethical perspective Catholic moral theology has recognized one source of conflict in its distinction between the objective moral order and the subjective. Objectively a particular act is morally wrong (e.g., drunkenness), but for this individual subject in these particular circumstances (e.g., an alcoholic) there is no subjective guilt or the guilt is greatly diminished. Philosophical ethics recognizes the same reality in its distinction between circumstances which justify an act (make it right) and circumstances which excuse an act (take away guilt without making it right).

There exist other sources of conflict situations in moral theology which can be reduced to three—eschatological tension, the presence of sin, and human finitude. Eschatological tension results from the fact that the fullness of the eschaton is not here, and in this pilgrim existence the eschatological exigencies cannot always be fully met. In this light I have argued against an absolute prohibition of divorce and remarriage.

The presence of sin in the world also causes some conflict situations. There can be no doubt that the presence of sin in the world has justified certain moral actions which would not be acceptable if there were no sin. Think of the justifications given for war, capital punishment, revolution, occult compensation. An older Catholic theology explicitly recognized that the justification of private property was grounded in the fact of original sin and not in human nature as such. In the light of my stance and contention that at times Catholic moral theology has not explicitly given enough importance to the reality of sin, it seems there might be other cases in which the presence of sin might justify an action which could not be justified if sin and its effects were not present. In the past I have referred to this as the theory of compromise. Such a theory is more a theological explanation of the source of the conflict and tension rather than a tightly reasoned ethical analysis of how it is to be applied in practice. Compromise was chosen to describe this reality in order to recognize the tension between justifying such actions because of the presence of sin and the Christian obligation to try to overcome sin and its effects. However, at times in this world sin and its presence cannot be overcome—a fact which the Catholic tradition has recognized in its discussion of war and private property; but perhaps a greater emphasis on the compromise aspect of these two ethical realities might have made us more cautious in dealing with them.

A third source of tension and conflict in establishing moral norms as preservers of values stems from human finitude. Values will at times conflict and clash because it is impossible to obtain or safeguard one value without losing or diminishing another value. At the very least moral theology should recognize the sources of the conflict situations which often arise in questions involving norms. However, the recognition of the different sources of conflict does not help to resolve the question of how norms are grounded and the question of modifications or exceptions in some norms that have been accepted as absolute in the manuals of moral theology.

In approaching the question of grounding norms much can be learned from a dialogue with contemporary philosophical ethics. The question is often phrased in terms of a deontological or teleological grounding of norms. According to the deontological grounding of norms certain actions are right or wrong no matter what the consequences. No matter how much good might result, suicide, for example, is always morally wrong. Such an approach has been called a Catholic position and certainly coincides with what has often been presented in Catholic philosophy and theology. However, some revisionist Catholic moralists maintain that norms are derived teleologically and this was true even for the Catholic understanding in the past. Norms were based on whether or not the particular action was judged good or evil for the human person and for society.

Many of the revisionist Catholic theologians, who have proposed a teleological grounding for norms, have employed an approach according to which commensurate reason can justify premoral or ontic evil and, thereby, have challenged some of the absolute norms defended in the manuals of moral theology. As a result some other Catholic theoreticians claim that such approaches are consequentialist, basing morality solely on the consequences of the action.[19]

An overview of the contemporary philosophical discussion about the grounding of norms indicates there are three different positions and not just two, but the terminology is confusing and not uniform. The one position is clearly deontological—some actions are always wrong no matter what the consequences. A second position is truly consequentialist, utilitarian, or strictly teleological and derives norms and the morality of actions solely on the basis of consequences. In this context there has been much debate about the difference between act and rule utilitarianism.

However, it is evident that there also exists a third position mediating between the two and called by different names including teleology and *prima facie* obligationalism.[20] This position rejects deontology but also disagrees with a strict teleology or consequentialism. In disagreement with strict consequentialists or utilitarians this middle position maintains the following three points: (1) moral obligations arise from elements other than consequences, e.g., promises, previous acts of gratitude or evil; (2) the good is not separate from the right; (3) the way in which the good or the evil is obtained by the agent and not just the end result is a moral consideration.

The existence of three different positions on the grounding of the moral norm indicates there are more than just two different approaches to this question. In my judgment the middle position is best described as a distinct approach based on a relationality-responsibility grounding of norms. Such a position grounds the norm on the basis of what is experienced as good for the person and for the total human society, and this on the basis of a relational criterion which gives importance to consequences but also gives moral value to aspects other than consequences.

In general, a relational grounding of the norm sees the norm as protecting and promoting values. Such an approach avoids the absolutism of a deontological approach and also the simplistic approach of a consequentialism which gives moral significance only to consequences. By highlighting the continued importance of the social dimension of human existence, such an approach recognizes that often norms are required for the good of all living together in human society.

The difference between my approach and that of Germain Grisez, a contemporary Catholic deontologist, helps to give a clearer understanding of how my approach works. According to Grisez there are eight basic human goods which the individual person can never directly go against.[21] My relational approach does not see the individual face to face with eight separate, basic goods but rather views the individual in multiple relationships with others and sees these goods as also related among themselves. At times there might be a conflict among these eight basic goods, and one might have to be sacrificed for other important values. In my methodology a relationality-responsibility model not only serves as the basic model of the Christian moral life but also grounds and establishes moral norms.

Conscience is the guide and director of the moral life of the individual. The understanding of conscience found in the manuals of moral theology can be criticized for being legalistic, minimalistic, overly rational, and too deductive. A better notion of conscience must be integrated within the understanding of the stance, model, and anthropology described above. For example, a relational model will not accept as primary the deontological understanding of conscience as the subjective norm of morality trying to conform to the objective norm of morality which is law in all its different aspects—divine, natural, and positive. Conscience is grounded in the subject, who is called to respond to the gospel message in the midst of the multiple relationships of human existence and thereby live out the thrust for authentic self-transcendence. Conscience thus partakes of the dynamism of the self-transcending subject.[22] The authentic life of the person as subject calls for self-transcendence which on the moral level reaches its fulfillment when the subject exists in a loving relationship with God, neighbor, the world, and self. An older faculty metaphysics situated conscience in the practical intellect. In my perspective conscience should be seen as an operation of the subject. In this way one can better integrate the creative and affective aspects of conscience and avoid a one-sided rationalism.

Conscience is the operation of the subject guiding and directing the moral life. Conscience is stimulated in many different ways—through parables, stories,[23] symbols, the liturgy, through the example of others as models, and through a myriad of life experiences. In its pursuit of values and self-transcendence the subject in many different ways comes to know, appreciate, love, and create the attitudes which should mark the life of the Christian. Conscience is seriously impoverished when it is reduced merely to a knowledge of the law, for its should be seen as an operation of the self-transcending subject trying to live out the fullness of the relationship with God, neighbor, the world, and self.

What about the decision of conscience about a particular action to be done here and now? In accord with a transcendental approach in the context of a relational model of ethics, the judgment of conscience is grounded ultimately in the self-transcending subject. The ultimate criterion of the truth of conscience is not conformity to the truth existing out there but is the self-transcendence of the human subject striving for authentic development. Authentic subjectivity is genuine objectivity.

The judgment of conscience is virtually unconditioned. The self-transcending subject with its thrust towards the true and the good constantly asks questions. The criterion of a true judgment exists when the subject rests at peace because there are no more pertinent questions to ask. The subject is always dealing with the data and reality before it and asking questions precisely to comprehend the moral meaning. Of course, there are dangers that the drive for authentic self-transcendence and the questioning based on it will be blunted and short-circuited, but the mature moral subject will be aware of these possible pitfalls and struggle against them.

The Christian tradition has talked about the peace and joy of conscience as being the sign of a good conscience. A transcendental theory grounds this peace and joy in the judgment of conscience as a virtually unconditioned in which the subject, constituted by its dynamic thrust toward self-transcendence, arrives at the true and the good and is at peace. The subject rests in the achievement of the true and the good. In this whole process the self is constantly asking questions about the entire moral act, end and circumstances, and takes all the steps which are appropriate in a discerning process including prayer, reflection, and counsel.

The dilemma of conscience has always arisen from the recognition that the individual must act in accord with one's own conscience, but conscience might be wrong. The generic limitations of conscience, especially in the light of the stance, are finitude and sinfulness. The person striving for true self-transcendence must be aware of these limitations and strive to overcome them. In this context, from a purely ethical viewpoint, which is obviously strengthened in the light of Catholic ecclesiology, one can see the importance of the church as a moral teacher because by definition the community of believers guided by the Spirit through various offices and charisms exists in diverse times and places and is aided in the struggle against sin. The church helps to overcome the twofold generic limitation of human conscience.

This study has attempted to sketch the method which should be employed in moral theology, especially in the light of the cultural and academic situation in the United States. On the basis of a presupposition recognizing great complexity in the moral life in general and in the systematic reflection on that experience, four general areas of reflection have been considered—the stance, the ethical model, anthropology, and norms and concrete decision making.

NOTES

1. John Tracy Ellis, "American Catholics and the Intellectual Life," *Thought* 30 (1955), 351-388.

2. See Ronald Stone, *Reinhold Niebuhr: Prophet to Politicians* (Nashville: Abingdon Press, 1971); also *Reinhold Niebuhr: His Religious, Social and Political Thought*, ed. Charles W. Kegley and Robert W. Bretall (New York: Macmillan Co., 1956).

3. James M. Gustafson, *Protestant and Roman Catholic Ethics: Prospects for Rapprochement* (Chicago: University of Chicago Press, 1978).

4. See, for example, *Ethics and Problems of the 21st Century*, ed. K.E. Goodpaster and K.M. Sayre (Notre Dame, Indiana: University of Notre Dame Press, 1979). On questions of justice much discussion has been sparked by John Rawls, *A Theory of Justice* (Cambridge, Mass.: Harvard University Press, 1971).

5. James Sellers,*Theological Ethics* (New York: Macmillan, 1966), pp. 29-68.

6. James M. Gustafson, *Christ and the Moral Life* (New York: Harper and Row, 1968), pp. 240-248.

7. The standard account of this movement remains Charles Howard Hopkins, *The Rise of the Social Gospel in American Protestantism, 1865-1915* (New Haven, Conn.: Yale University Press, 1940).

8. Paul Lehmann, *Ethics in a Christian Context* (New York: Harper and Row, 1963); Lehmann, *The Transfiguration of Politics* (New York: Harper and Row, 1975).

9. Jürgen Moltmann, *The Theology of Hope* (New York: Harper and Row, 1967); Moltmann, *The Crucified God* (New York: Harper and Row, 1974); Johannes B. Metz, *Theology of*

the World (New York: The Seabury Press, 1969); Metz, "The Future in the Memory of Suffering," *New Concilium* 76 (1972), 9-25.

10. H. Richard Niebuhr, *Christ and Culture* (New York: Harper Torchbook, 1956).

11. The way in which moral theology employs the scriptures in moral theology constitutes another very significant methodological question. I distinguish different ways in which the scriptures have an impact on the four levels discussed here— stance, ethical model, anthropology, and concrete actions and norms. For a recent discussion of this question in American Christian ethics, see Bruce C. Birch and Larry L. Rasmussen, *Bible and Ethics in the Christian Life* (Minneapolis, Minn.: Augsburg Publishing House, 1976). These authors do not consider any Catholic literature coming from outside the United States.

12. H. Richard Niebuhr, *The Responsible Self: An Essay in Christian Moral Philosophy* (New York: Harper and Row, 1963).

13. Daniel C. Maguire, *The Moral Choice* (Garden City, New York: Doubleday, 1978).

14. Kohlberg has published his stages of moral development in many different places. For a recent elucidation, see Lawrence Kohlberg, "The Implications of Moral Stages for Adult Education," *Religious Education* 72, 2 (March-April 1977), 183-201.

15. Illustrative of this critical approach are the following: Paul J. Philibert, "Conscience: Developmental Perspectives from Rogers and Kohlberg," *Horizons* 6 (1979), 1-25; Walter E. Conn, "Post-conventional Morality: An Exposition and Critique of Lawrence Kohlberg's Analysis of Moral Development in the Adolescent and Adult," *Lumen Vitae* 30 (1975), 213-230.

16. A significant factor on the American scene is the interest by Protestant ethicians in the subject and in character. See James M. Gustafson, *Christian Ethics and the Community* (Philadelphia: Pilgrim Press, 1971), pp. 151-216; also in his *Christ and the Moral Life;* Stanley Hauerwas, *Character and the Christian Life: A Study in Theological Ethics* (San Antonio, Texas: Trinity University Press, 1975).

17. The universal destiny of the goods of creation to serve the needs of all has been highlighted in more recent statements of

the hierarchical magisterium; but John A. Ryan, the leading figure in American Catholic social ethics in the first half of the twentieth century, insisted on such a first principle in his discussions of the goods of creation and the system of private property. See John A. Ryan, *Distributive Justice* (New York: Macmillan, 1916), pp. 56-60. See also Reginald G. Bender, "The Doctrine of Private Property in the Writings of Monsignor John A. Ryan" (S.T.D. dissertation, The Catholic University of America, 1973).

18. For a book of readings in English of significant articles originally written on this topic in various languages, see *Readings in Moral Theology, No. 1: Moral Norms and the Catholic Tradition,* ed. Charles E. Curran and Richard A. McCormick (New York: Paulist Press, 1979). On the American scene Richard A. McCormick has done the most to carry on a dialogue on this question of norms both with Catholic moral theologians throughout the world and with Protestant and philosophical ethicians in the United States. See especially his "Notes on Moral Theology" which appear regularly in *Theological Studies* and also *Doing Evil to Achieve Good: Moral Choice in Conflict Situations,* ed. Richard A. McCormick and Paul Ramsey (Chicago: Loyola University Press, 1978).

19. John R. Connery, "Morality of Consequences: A Theological Appraisal," *Theological Studies* 34 (1973), 396-414; reprinted in *Readings in Moral Theology, No. 1,* pp. 244-266.

20. This third or mediating position is held by a large number of philosophers. See, for example, Rawls, *A Theory of Justice,* pp. 25ff; William K. Frankena, *Ethics* (Englewood Cliffs, New Jersey: Prentice-Hall, 1963), pp. 13ff.

21. Germain Grisez, *Abortion: The Myths, the Realities and the Arguments* (New York: Corpus Books, 1970), pp. 311-321; Germain Grisez and Russell Shaw, *Beyond the New Morality: The Responsibilities of Freedom* (Notre Dame, Indiana: University of Notre Dame Press, 1974). For his critique of what he calls consequentialism, see Germain Grisez, "Against Consequentialism," *The American Journal of Jurisprudence* 23 (1978), 21-72.

22. For a detailed development of this notion of conscience, see Walter E. Conn, *Conscience: Development and Self-Transcendence* (Birmingham, Alabama: Religious Education Press, 1981).

23. For a strong insistence on the importance of story, see Stanley Hauerwas, with Richard Bondi and David B. Burrell, *Truthfulness and Tragedy: Further Investigations into Christian Ethics* (Notre Dame, Indiana: University of Notre Dame Press, 1977), especially pp. 15-98.

4. Three Methodological
Issues in Moral Theology

This chapter will focus on three important issues in moral theology—the discipline of moral theology, anthropology, and the question of a distinctively Christian ethic. These important issues have been frequently raised in contemporary literature and surfaced as the most significant issues at a conference on moral theology held at the University of Notre Dame in April of 1980.[1]

I. The Discipline of Moral Theology

There seems to be general agreement today that moral theology must consider more than questions of judgments about particular actions and norms. Undoubtedly these are important questions which moral theology cannot neglect, but they do not constitute the only, or even the most important, questions for the discipline. Too often in the past the manualist approach has tended to deal only with specific actions and norms. Both history and contemporary dialogue show that the agenda of moral theology must be broader. Before the advent of the *Institutiones theologiae moralis* in the seventeenth century, moral theology had a much more inclusive scope. Unfortunately, speculative moral theology became divorced from practical moral theology, and the impression was often given that the only aspect of moral theology was the judgment about the morality of particular actions.

Classical moral theology traditionally had recognized the importance and significance of concerns such as the end or the goal of the moral life, the character and virtues of the individual Christian, the values and ideals that are to be incarnated in our world, in our society, and in our lives. Today anyone studying moral theology recognizes the need for a more comprehensive approach which understands moral theology as reflecting on the Christian life in all its dimensions. An exclusively act-centered moral theology remains incomplete and insufficient. The previous chapter has discussed four different levels of concern in moral theology—stance, ethical model, anthropology, and decision making and norms.

Moral theology by its very nature has a foundational twofold relationship which helps to describe its nature and function—a relationship to the church and to systematic reasoning or academe. By definition moral theology involves systematic, thematic, and critical reflection on the Christian moral life. Moral theology is an academic discipline. Moral theology is a systematic discipline in the service of the church. Both these aspects of moral theology are important; at times the dual relationship causes tension for moral theology and for moral theologians. In addition, dangers lurk when the healthy tension between the two aspects no longer exists.

As a discipline moral theology involves second-order discourse. Scientific and methodological rigor are very important for the development of moral theology. Not all reflection on the Christian moral life involves moral theology as such. Most importantly, the contemporary needs of the discipline remind us practitioners that moral theology must be in dialogue with many other disciplines today. Above all, moral theology must be seen as a constitutive part of Christian theology. Too often in the past moral theology has been separated from dogmatic or systematic theology. But moral theology is also systematic theology. Furthermore, the renewal of moral theology in the Catholic Church has recognized the fact that moral theology must be nourished by the Word of God in the scriptures. There has been much literature in the last few

years about the place of the scriptures in moral theology
and the way in which the discipline of moral theology
employs the scriptures.[2] In addition, moral theology
recognizes the need to be conversant with other ethical
theory both in religious ethics and in philosophical
ethics. Moral theology necessarily is in dialogue with the
human and social sciences such as anthropology, economics, psychology, and sociology. A very significant
methodological question concerns the way in which
moral theology integrates and uses the empirical sciences.

The relationship of moral theology to academe underscores the second-order nature of the discourse of moral
theology. It does not follow that moral theology must
necessarily be done only in a university context or setting,
but such a setting is an appropriate place for moral
theology. In such an environment moral theology can
carry on its systematic reflection with scientific and
methodological rigor and at the same time be nourished
and enriched by a living dialogue with other disciplines.
History reminds us of the decline of moral theology which
resulted from its isolation from other disciplines and from
its too great concern merely for practical questions based
on the narrow function of preparing confessors for the
sacrament of penance.

However, there are dangers that arise from an exaggera-
tion of the academic and scientific nature of moral
theology. The first danger comes from an overemphasis
which forgets about the church-related aspect of the
discipline. Moral theology exists in the service of the
church. The nature of moral theology as systematic and
critical reflection can never separate it from its matrix in
the believing Christian community. To associate moral
theology with academe more than with the church
involves a great distortion. One must admit that moral
theology is not a liberal discipline in the sense that it is
seeking knowledge only for its own sake. The knowledge
that it seeks is always in the service of the church and of the
believing Christian community.

The relationship to the church also prevents moral
theology from becoming academic in the most pejorative

sense of the term, as being esoteric and not related to the lived reality of human Christian experience. Perhaps a comparison with philosophical ethics will make the point. Until recently many philosophers have not been interested in the specific questions facing humanity and human beings in our world. In the area of medical ethics a practicing doctor has complained that the ethicists are not dealing with the everyday problems faced by doctors.[3] Undoubtedly the philosopher is more intrigued by the interesting cases which bring out a particular point, but often these cases are quite contrived and totally extraordinary if not altogether unreal: for example, a promise made on an isolated island to a dying person or a question of judicial murder. A relationship to the life of the church has kept Catholic moral theology "practical" in the sense of dealing with the everyday questions of human and Christian existence. The opposite danger of becoming too practical and neglecting the theoretical and methodological aspects of systematic reflection has already been pointed out, but a recognition of service to the church can and should keep moral theology in touch with the lived realities facing the believing community.

The relationship of moral theology to the life of the church and the community of believers is obvious, for the content or subject matter of the discipline is the Christian life itself with all its ramifications. The church needs moral theologians and must encourage the growth of moral theology. Strange as it might sound, I fear that the importance and role of moral theology in the church might be exaggerated at the expense of other important functions. Moral theology serves the church by doing well its own task of thematic and systematic reflection.

In the past I think moral theologians have exercised too great a role in the life of the church. The past importance and inflation of the role of moral theology in the church was based on the importance of the moral systems and the emergence of probabilism within the context of a somewhat legalistic moral theology. Moral theologians were often called upon to determine if a particular position was probable in practice. If it were probable, then individual

Christians could follow such an opinion in practice. Probability in practice usually meant extrinsically probable, that is, recognized as probable by six theologians of repute. This function of moral theologians has rightly been de-emphasized in the light of a changing understanding both of moral theology and of the Christian moral life. Today the responsible and conscientious decision making of the individual receives greater emphasis.

In the present and future, moral theology can best serve the church by recognizing both its importance and its limitations. As second-order, systematic discourse, moral theology is very important for the life of the church, but it must be distinguished from other connected realities, especially the living of the Christian life, the preaching of the good news, and the moral formation of the Christian community.

Moral theology is not the same as the living of the Christian moral life. One might be tempted to think that the living follows from the theoretical and systematic understanding of moral theology, but such is not the case. Practical experience reminds us that many people who have never studied moral theology have lived exemplary lives. The Christian theologian always recognizes the difficulty in measuring, evaluating, and even comparing the response of people to the gospel in their daily lives, but our common experience reminds us that living the message of Jesus does not require that one be a moral theologian. Our own honesty and humility as Christians remind us who practice moral theology that there are many other people in the Christian community whose witness to the gospel in their daily life puts us to shame. Lately it has become commonplace to criticize some approaches to Christian spirituality as exemplified in *The Imitation of Christ*. However, we should all agree with the author of *The Imitation of Christ* that it is much more important to live out the meaning of love and compassion than it is to define the terms.

Theology today often stresses praxis.[4] Many contemporary moral theologians are stressing the nature of moral theology as reflection on our own Christian experience. Note that experience comes first, and the reflection follows on it. Many can and do live out the Christian moral life without reflecting on that experience in a thematic and systematic way.[5]

There is a related and significant question as to whether one can be a moral theologian and not be a believer in the gospel. I conclude it is possible for one to be involved in the discipline of moral theology and not be a believer. I am thinking of a number of people who are deeply involved in Christian ethics but are not believing Christians. However, at the very minimum the personal integrity of the one who is both believer and moral theologian calls for such a person to live out these two closely related commitments involving one's life and one's systematic reflection.

The function of moral theology also differs from the function of preaching the good news in the Christian community. There must be an intimate connection between theology and preaching, but they are different realities and should not become confused. Preaching tends to be first-order discourse and does not involve the systematic reflection which is the nature of the discipline of moral theology.

Moral theology plays a part, but only a part, in the moral formation of the Christian community. In fact, the role of moral theology is not the most prominent. Moral formation takes place in many different ways and is heavily influenced by parents and family. Liturgy, preaching, discussions, and classes all have a role in the moral formation of the community. A very important and significant role is played by the example and witness of Christian people themselves. In the past Catholics heavily emphasized the example of the saints, but unfortunately there has been a tendency to forget the importance of such witness and example within the last few decades. Moral theology has a contribution to make in all these areas of moral living, preaching, and formation, but its expertise lies on the level of systematic and thematic reflection, and its contribution is in terms of theory, understanding, and critique.

The question of the precise relationship in the church between moral theology and the hierarchical teaching office continues to be a very significant issue. This topic has been discussed in chapter one, but a few practical comments are in order.

Currently in the United States there exists a great deal of tension between bishops and moral theologians. Although I believe that some tension should always be present, nonetheless there is need for a much better relationship than now exists. We all know that there is a list of Catholic moral theologians who for all practical purposes are blacklisted from doing work for the institutional church and are not considered safe. In my somewhat prejudiced judgment, the good of the church suffers when some theologians are arbitrarily cut off from contributing to the ongoing work of the church. Bishops must be free to choose their collaborators for any number of different reasons, but entire groups of people should not be arbitrarily excluded.

One of the virtues of academe has been its supposed openness to all sides and all opinions. If there is an attempt within the church not to listen to all sides, one would hope that such a situation would not exist in academe. Unfortunately, academe has also failed to be open to all points of view. In June, 1979, a conference on Catholic moral theology was held at the Catholic University of America to which only scholars of an identifiably conservative bent (usually most evident in terms of one's position on *Humanae vitae*) were invited to give presentations. However, the Notre Dame symposium was no better. There were no papers presented at Notre Dame by people who gave addresses at the Catholic University conference last year. We who practice the discipline of moral theology have an obligation to make sure that we are willing to be in dialogue with all those involved in the dicipline. Both the service to the church and the good of the dicipline itself suffer when there are two different camps of moral theologians who are not in dialogue and communication.

One final comment on the discipline of moral theology concerns the practitioners of the discipline. It appears that some people have shied away from entering the field of Catholic moral theology in the last few years. The questions and problems are so vast that we need all the competent help we can have in trying to do our work. Hopefully this situation will improve in the future. In addition to the problem of the quantity and quality of moral theologians in general, there also remains a great problem that our ranks are primarily, if not exclusively, white, middle-class males. Both the church and the discipline of moral theology will be helped if there is a greater representation of women, Hispanics, blacks, and other minority groups. We as practitioners in the field can wash our hands and claim that the people working in the discipline are not our responsibility, but such a solution is the easy, and perhaps the irresponsible, way out. We can do a number of things both individually and as a professional group to encourage and help women, Hispanics, and blacks to enter the field.

II. Anthropology

The second major area of reflection concerns anthropology, which constitutes a most significant issue in moral theology. Chapter three insisted·on a relationality-responsibility model for moral theology. The Notre Dame conference seemed to generate a similar consensus. The human person must be seen in terms of multiple relationships with God, neighbor, self, and nature or the world.

The relationship of the person to God grounds many important considerations in moral theology. The dialogical character of the Christian moral life has been underscored in the renewal of Catholic moral theology and is well illustrated in the pioneering and continuing work of Bernard Häring.[6] A perennial temptation in moral theology has been pelagianism or semipelagianism—the heretical position that human beings save themselves by their own efforts. By seeing the human person in terms of a relationship with God, the gifted character of Christian existence and life becomes more evident. If the Christian sees life primarily as a gift of God in Jesus, then the primary response of the Christian is one of gratitude and praise. Immediately the connection between the liturgy and the moral life of the Christian becomes evident.[7] Prayer also assumes an important place in the moral life of the Christian. Such emphases have too often been forgotten in Catholic moral theology.

A second advantage of the multiple-relationship model concerns the political, social, and cosmic dimensions of the moral life. A tendency to play down the social and political dimensions has frequently been associated with some Catholic moral theology. The multiple-relational concept of anthropology at least provides a firm basis for considering the social and political dimensions of human existence. No longer can the individual be concerned only about one's self. Other reasons supporting the political and social dimensions of the Christian life will be mentioned later. Our contemporary world is more than ever conscious of the interrelationship which binds us to all other human beings. Moral theology needs an anthropological basis to incorporate such a broad vision and horizon.

By mentioning the relationship to nature and the world an important aspect of human existence is underlined. Too often in the past the ecological problem has been dismissed or not even raised. Especially in the light of a developing and almost omnipotent technology, human beings forgot about our relationship to and dependence upon the natural world.

Reflection on contemporary existence often comes to the conclusion that too often in the immediate past human beings have exercised an autonomy and arrogance that have been the cause of much evil in our society. In terms of traditional moral theology, human beings have too often been tempted by the capital sin of pride and have refused to recognize their dependence and limitations. The arrogance of power and of selfish autonomy has been rampant in all aspects of human life. This contemporary consciousness prevalent in the world in general and in theological reflection differs quite a bit from the consciousness that pervaded our society less than two decades ago. Harvey Cox epitomized this other approach by insisting in the 1960s that the primary sin of human beings is not pride, because of which they try to play God and do too much, but rather *acedia* or sloth, because of which human beings do not take responsibility for the world in which we live.[8] Events of the last few years have chastened the utopian optimism of the middle 1960s. We are more conscious than ever of the evils and problems created by autonomous individuals, corporations, and nations aggressively pursuing their selfish and narrow goals.

In this context, some contemporary theologians, including David Burrell at the Notre Dame conference, have insisted on the need to stress the human being as a responder and not as an initiator. Receptivity, gratitude, and interdependence must characterize contemporary Christians rather than initiative, autonomy, and independence. However, there is need for some nuancing. A relational model and the need to overcome the dangers of false autonomy should not go so far as to forget the place of true autonomy, which can and should exist in human beings living in interdependence. An anthropology based on the indvidual's multiple relationships underlines the dangers of a false autonomy and independence, calls for the individual to recognize the web of dependencies in human existence, and yet does not deny a rightful place for creativity and initiative, especially in the service of these various relationships. Just as two decades ago theology erred by overstressing the greatness and autonomy of the individual, so too today we must avoid a reaction that gives no place to a proper creativity and initiative in the midst of the multiple relationships which define and characterize our existence.

There are many other aspects of anthropology which cannot be touched upon here, but a significant amount of emphasis in Catholic moral theology in the last few years has been given to the person understood as a self-transcending subject. The philosophical basis for such an approach comes from transcendental Thomism, especially as developed by Lonergan and Rahner. In moral theology Joseph Fuchs has employed such a notion, and Timothy O'Connell develops such a concept of the person in his *Principles for a Catholic Morality.*[9]

Many contemporary Catholic moral theologians employ the understanding of the person as a self-transcending subject as the foundation for a theory of fundamental option. This theory distinguishes between the core freedom of the individual and freedom of choice, transcendental freedom and categorical freedom. Freedom of choice refers to the particular categorical choices we make to do this particular act or another; core freedom involves the transcendental self-commitment of the person in the depths of one's own existence. The self-commitment of the person in transcendental freedom is not an isolated individual act existing by itself but rather is copresent with the categorical choices we make. The categorical choices concern the particular objects of choice, whereas the transcendental refers to the subject's disposition of oneself. Very often our actions remain only on the categorical level and do not involve the basic core freedom of the person. The fundamental option theory is often employed to explain the difference between mortal and venial sin. Mortal sin involves a change in the fundamental option, in the basic commitment of the subject on the level of the core or transcendental freedom of the person.[10]

The understanding of the person as a self-transcending subject has often served as a basis in contemporary Catholic moral theology for explaining growth and development in the Christian life. Historically, Protestant theology has been fearful of speaking about growth and development in the Christian life for fear that it deflates the gratuitousness of God's gracious gift, but an acceptance of growth is not incompatible with Protestant self-understanding.[11] Catholic theology must recognize the pelagian tint of some of its approaches to growth, but the reality of growth in the Christian life cannot be denied. In the last few years there has been a widely accepted thrust in Catholic moral theology to explain growth and development in terms of conversion. Bernard Häring has rooted the concept of conversion in the basic biblical call to a change of heart. Conversion, or *metanoia,* is a fundamental reality in the preaching of Jesus and of the early church. Häring has insisted especially on the concept of continual conversion, which has its foundation in eschatology. The individual Christian, like the whole Christian community, is on pilgrimage. The Christian should continually grow and strive to be evermore open to the gift of God in Jesus and evermore faithful to the convenant promise. The sacraments are above all signs and symbols of conversion as God's gracious gift and our continuing response.[12]

Bernard Lonergan on the basis of his transcendental Thomism insists that reflection on the ongoing process of conversion is the real foundation of a renewed theology. Conversion is an ongoing process which is concrete and dynamic, personal, communal, and historical. Thus, conversion for Lonergan is foundational for theology itself. Lonergan discusses three conversions—intellectual, moral, and religious—all of which are modalities of self-transcendence. Religious conversion involves a total being-in-love as the efficacious ground of all self-transcendence.[13]

The emphasis on the person as a self-transcending subject has opened Catholic moral theology to dialogue with humanistic psychologists and their approaches to growth and development in the human subject. Much attention has been given to Piaget, Erikson, and Kohlberg by Catholic moral theologians.[14] Dialogue with these psychologists does not necessarily involve complete acceptance of their approaches as is evident in recent theological writing which tends to be more critical of Kohlberg than the first reactions to his theory of moral development.[15]

In contemporary Catholic moral theology there seems to be heavy emphasis on both a relational anthropology and on an understanding of the person as a self-transcending subject. As the previous chapter has shown, I, too, have sympathies for both these approaches and want to attempt to bring them together. Some relational approaches do not give enough importance to the subject. On the other hand the acceptance of a relational concept can and should modify somewhat the existing transcendental approaches. The danger with a transcendental understanding by itself is the failure to give enough importance to the political and social dimensions of human existence. An emphasis on relationality can serve as a corrective to the overemphasis on the subject in the transcendental approach.

A second modification to the transcendental concept involves a greater appreciation of the reality of sin in the Christian moral life. Although both Lonergan and Häring talk about the centrality of conversion, their approaches are quite different. Lonergan grounds conversion in the various levels of self-transcendence of the subject, whereas Häring grounds conversion in the realities of grace and sin. At the very minimum the transcendental approach must give greater importance to the reality of sin.

A third modification of the transcendental understanding affects the concept of growth. In addition to the growth of the subject discussed in much of the contemporary psychological literature, a more relational emphasis can understand growth in terms of human relationships such as the growth in friendships or in marriage. Much work remains to be done in developing both the relationality and the transcendental approaches and in trying to bring together the best aspects of both.

III. A Distinctively Christian Ethics and Morality

The third area of reflection might best be described as the question about a distinctively Christian morality and ethics. Let me begin with an observation about the Notre Dame meeting. This conference was the "churchiest" meeting I have attended as a moral theologian in the last decade. The titles of the first four papers illustrate this "churchy" aspect—"Faith: Source of Christian Ethics," "The Biblical Basis of Christian Ethics," "The Authority of Tradition," and "A Community Ethics." Two of the first four speakers—Stanley Hauerwas and John Howard Yoder—were characterized by Edward Malloy in his paper as employing a mode of the church as a community of formation—a model closely related to what Troeltsch called the sect type. John Howard Yoder has creatively employed this understanding of church in his many writings interpreting and applying his own Mennonite background.[16] Stanley Hauerwas has observed that the church is not called to build culture or supply the moral tone of civilization; rather, the church must become a community separate from the predominant culture and preach that the kingdom of God has come close in the person and work of Jesus. The church teaches and proclaims the truth of the kingdom.[17] In this model the function of the church is to present its own witness, which then can show up the pretension, hypocrisy, and shallowness of much of contemporary life. The primary role of the Christian ethicist in this approach is to help in the formation of the members of the Christian community by nurturing within the community the Christian story and its ramifications for life and decision making.

In my judgment a most significant lack in the first part of the Notre Dame conference was the absence of eschatology. The very title of the conference shows the lack of eschatology: "Remembering and Reforming: Towards a Constructive Christian Ethics." There is no looking forward in the title but only a looking backward. Remembering almost necessarily entails an exclusive emphasis on the community of God's people and the events that happen in that community. Eschatology in a number of ways helps to overcome a too narrow emphasis on the Christian community and the church. Eschatology points ahead and allows us to consider the present not only in the light of the past but also in view of a wider and broader future involving the final consummation of God's plan

for the world. Such a view of eschatology is intimately
connected with the notion of the reign or the kingdom of
God. The reign or the kingdom of God is much more
inclusive than the church. Eschatology also serves as a
basis for criticism within the church. The Catholic
ecclesiology sanctioned at the Second Vatican Council
speaks of the church not as a perfect society but as a
pilgrim community. The pilgrim church on its journey to
the fullness of the kingdom is not totally perfect and
without spot. In a true sense the church will always be a
sinful church and never perfect, especially in the light of
the eschatological fullness of the kingdom.

A narrow ecclesiology too often forgets that the Christian belongs to many communities and not merely the
church community. In and through these other communities the individual Christian is formed and shaped. The
church community itself can and should learn from these
other different communities existing in our world. The
church must also be critical about herself and her own
history. A selective remembering too often forgets the sin,
arrogance, and infidelity that so often affects the church in
its pilgrimage through history. The fear of a triumphalism of the church is ever present in a narrow ecclesiology.

All these reasons point to the heavily "churchy atmosphere" that pervaded much of the conference. No Christian can deny the importance and the role of the church as
the community of God's people saved by Jesus and
animated by the Spirit, but the concept of the kingdom is
broader than the concept of church. Christian ethics must
also be interested in life in the world outside the ecclesial
parameters. Within such a narrow ecclesiological context
it is only natural that the distinctive aspect of Christian
morality and Christian ethics is heavily accented.

The question of the distinctiveness of Christian ethics
has come to the fore as a result of some recent developments in Catholic moral theology. The renewal of moral
theology, beginning in the 1950s, reacted against both the
scope of the manuals of moral theology and their theological methodology. The manuals used a natural law
methodology (based on human nature as known by

human reason) and concentrated on training confessors to judge the existence, number, and gravity of sins. The renewal insisted that the aim of moral theology must be not merely to point out sin and the lower limits of the Christian life but to explain the whole Christian life including the universal call to holiness. A minimalistic and legalistic moral theology did not give sufficient attention to the total moral existence of the Christian and completely forgot the dynamism and growth which must characterize the Christian life. From the methodological perspective, the renewal has emphasized the role of the scriptures as the soul of all theology, including moral theology, and the specifically Christian aspects of life in the Spirit and discipleship.

There exists a great methodological gulf between *Pacem in terris,* the encyclical of Pope John XXIII published in 1963, and *Gaudium et spes,* the Pastoral Constitution on the Church in the Modern World issued by the Second Vatican Council in 1965.[18] *Pacem in terris* bases its approach on a natural law methodology. In the opening paragraphs Pope John speaks about the order which the Creator of the world has placed in the world and the law imprinted on the human heart which conscience reveals. On the basis of this order and this law human beings are taught how to conduct their mutual relations (par. 1-7). Note that no reference is made to specifically and distinctively Christian themes such as peace as the gift of the Risen Lord to his disciples.

Gaudium et spes, on the other hand, uses a different methodological approach. Part one of this document deals with the more general questions of the meaning of human persons, of human activity, and of human communities and tries to understand all of these in the light of creation, sin, and redemption. There is a conscious effort to speak from a distinctively Christian perspective and to avoid understanding the natural as an almost autonomous order unaffected by sin and grace. Part two of *Gaudium et spes* treats more specific questions such as marriage and the family, cultural and political matters, in the light of the gospel and of human experience.[19] In the

light of this newer methodological approach the question
of a distinctively Christian ethic arises.

In the Notre Dame conference the different positions on
this question were well illustrated by the approach of
Yoder and Hauerwas on the one hand and McCormick on
the other. Whereas Yoder and Hauerwas stress the distinctive character of Christian ethics and its differences from
other human ethics, McCormick insists that the concrete
behavioral norms are not radically mysterious. The
concrete moral implications of our being-in-Christ can
per se be known by human reasoning and insight, and
these moral norms apply to all persons precisely as human
persons.

The differences which surfaced at the Notre Dame
symposium also appear in the contemporary literature. In
his book *The Moral Choice* Daniel Maguire argues that
human decision making is the same for all—Christians
and non-Christians alike. Maguire's wheel of moral
decision making, with its hub representing the questions
involved in the expository stage of ethics and its spokes
representing the evaluational stage of ethics, is the same
for all whether they are believers or not.[20] A considerably
different approach to Christian ethics is taken by Hauerwas in his written work with his emphasis on the
distinctive Christian story and narrative which shapes and
forms the individual believer and the believing community. At the very least both authors (as somewhat illustrative
of their respective positions) deal with the aspect of the
question which is most compatible with the position
taken. Hauerwas deals especially with the character and
attitudes that characterize Christian existence. Obviously
here one would expect to speak about distinctive Christian attitudes and approaches. Maguire in his book does
not deal with questions of character, attitude, or dispositions but rather concentrates on the way in which concrete
decisions are made. In his response at the Notre Dame
conference Maguire did recognize a place for explicitly
Christian understandings of issues such as character and
dispositions. The precise differences between the two
approaches can only be known when they address the full

spectrum of the considerations of moral theology including the more general questions of values, goals, attitudes, character, and dispositions as well as the concrete moral decision-making process. Hauerwas, however, even in discussing some concrete decision making on specific moral questions facing society maintains that the Christian approach is different.[21]

The question of a distinctively Christian ethics is primarily a theological issue and involves many theological considerations. Rather than attempt to evaluate and criticize the positions of others, I will propose my own approach. The significant theological issues involved include revelation, soteriology, Christology, eschatology, and ecclesiology. These different theological aspects will definitely color one's whole approach to moral theology.

Revelation is much broader than the scriptures. There is something that exists behind or, if you want, before the story and the narrative of God's covenant with his people and the founding of the Christian community by Jesus. God's gracious self-communication is offered to all human beings. The scriptures are a privileged record of God's saving revelation, but in no way do they exhaust that revelation.

Intimately connected with revelation is soteriology. God's saving self-gift is somehow or other offered to all human beings. Grace is not confined just to the church community. These two approaches to revelation and to soteriology thus qualify what is to be said about the Chistian story. There is something more original than the Christian story from which it is derived, and the story is not going to be as distinctive and unique as it might first appear.

The implications for Christology are obvious. Jesus is the sacrament and the mediator through whom the Father comes to human beings and at the same time the one through whom believers return to the Father. As important and significant as is the role and function of Jesus, God's salvific gift can and does exist outside the pale of the explicitly Christian. One way to explain this Christology is in terms of Karl Rahner's anonymous Christianity, but this is not necessarily the only way to develop and explain such a general approach to Christology and its relationship to revelation and soteriology.

Eschatology has already been discussed in terms of its relationship to the future consummation of creation, its pointing to the kingdom as more inclusive than the church, and its recognition of the not-yet character of our present existence. Some of the implications of such an eschatology for ecclesiology have already been mentioned. This approach to eschatology and to ecclesiology points to the political and social aspects of moral theology. According to the often-quoted statement of the Synod of Bishops in 1971: "Action on behalf of justice and participation in the transformation of the world fully appear to us as a constitutive dimension of the preaching of the gospel, or, in other words, of the Church's mission for the redemption of the human race and its liberation from every oppressive situation" (par. 6).[22]

In my understanding of eschatology and ecclesiology the social mission of the gospel and of the church is rooted in the fact that the salvific plan of God is destined to embrace all of creation. The church is at the service of the world and the kingdom. The saving gift of God's love is destined to free all God's creatures from sin, including its social dimensions of oppression, poverty, and injustice. The role of the church and the function of its moral theology refer not merely to the life of the community of the church but to the life of the world itself. The church, its ministry, and its theological reflection have too often failed to recognize that action on behalf of justice and participation in the transformation of the world are essential aspects of the gospel message and of the mission of the church.

Latin American liberation theology is the best known example of such an understanding of the role and function of the church in struggling against all forms of oppression to transform the world. However, I hasten to mention that I have some friendly amendments to modify aspects of liberation theology. The eschatology mentioned above reminds us of the not-yet character of our earthly existence. We will never be completely successful in our struggle for justice and liberation, for the fullness of the kingdom as God's gracious gift will never be present in this world. Determining what is to be done in concrete situations remains a very complex reality, and often there will be no one concrete Christian solution to the problems that face us. Action on behalf of the transformation of the world is a constitutive dimension of the gospel, but it is not the only essential aspect of the gospel and of the mission of the church. Likewise, Christians must avoid the temptation of a triumphalism which forgets that there are many non-Christians who have been and are passionately devoted to the transformation of the world. In addition, there is a place in life and in theology for contemplative reason as well as critical reason.

The eschatological and ecclesiological bases for this social mission of the church cohere with a relational understanding of anthropology which recognizes our relationships to others and to the world. In the light of our past history perhaps the greatest challenge the church faces today in the United States is to put flesh and bones on the statement of the international Synod of Bishops. Already there are attempts in theory to de-emphasize that statement by saying that a constitutive dimension of the gospel refers to an integral but not an essential part of the gospel.[23] I disagree. The significance of this statement of the Synod of Bishops is astounding. On every level of church—local, diocesan, national, and worldwide—an essential element of the church is missing if there is not action on behalf of the transformation of the world. To have church it is not enough to have liturgical assemblies. There must be social mission as an essential part of being church.

In the light of this background one can approach the question of a distinctively Christian ethics. Some clarifications are in order. About ten years ago I wrote what apparently was the first article dealing directly with this subject in this country: "Is There a Distinctively Christian Social Ethic?"[24] In hindsight it is evident that I dealt primarily with morality rather than with ethics. Ethics refers to a systematic and thematic discipline, whereas morality refers to the actions that one does or the dispositions one has. As a discipline Christian ethics or moral theology is distinctive at least in the sense that it has its own distinctive and exclusive sources such as the scriptures, tradition, and the life of the church which are peculiar to Christian ethics. Chapter three has outlined a methodology for moral theology which indicates its distinctively Christian character. I disagree with the statement occasionally made by O'Connell that philosophical ethics and moral theology are the same.[25]

The word "distinctive" also can be confusing. Without doubt there is something distinctive about Christian ethics or Christian morality, but the further question concerns whether there is something exclusive about Christian ethics or morality which does not and cannot belong to other ethics or moralities.[26] Another helpful distinction refers to morality which is required for all (sometimes called essentialist) and morality which is specific to particular individuals (sometimes called existentialist).[27]

In my judgment Christian ethics or moral theology is a species of ethics. Ethics can be philosophical or religious. The Christian aspect does not change the nature of ethics. Questions about the way in which norms are developed, the decision-making process, the relationship of dispositions and character to acts, the question of values, goals, and ideals are the same basic questions asked in all ethical inquiry. At the very minimum what Christian does to "ethics" is to specify it to recognize the distinctive Christian sources of ethics. But moral theology or Christian ethics remains as a species or type of ethics and does not become something other than ethics.

What about the relationship of Christian morality to other morality, or what might be called the content of ethics? At first sight one might tend to think there is a great difference between Christian morality and non-Christian morality. However, the theological presuppositions discussed above point in the opposite direction. God's salvific self-communication is revealed and offered to all human beings. History and experience remind us that non-Christians have embraced self-sacrificing love, given their lives for others, and rejected all forms of violence. I deny that there is an exclusive Christian content to morality in terms of either the concrete decisions made by Christians or the proximate attitudes, goals, and dispositions they propose as normative for human existence. Non-Christians can and do share these same values, norms, goals, attitudes, dispositions, and acts. An exclusive Christian intentionality might explain the reason for the Christian's willingness to give one's life for another or to share the goods of creation with other human beings, but non-Christians can and do arrive at the same conclusions and cherish the same attitudes and values. Here we are talking about essentialist morality.

Notice that my approach to this question is somewhat abstract and even universal. One can never forget that in our world and culture many non-Christians do not share these same values and norms, but in practice many Christians also do not live according to these values and goals. Sin is present not only in the world but also in the church. Thus the material content of Christian morality involving norms, values, goals, attitudes, dispositions, and acts cannot claim to be exclusively Christian because non-Christians can and do share them.

Recent official church documents seem to agree with this perspective. The Christian and the fully human, the truly human, and the perfectly human are the same according to the Pastoral Constitution on the Church in the Modern World.[28] Pope Paul VI in *Populorum progressio* (par. 14-21) speaks of a transcendent humanism and a new humanism.[29]

What does this understanding of the relationship between Christian morality and truly human morality (understood in the sense of essential morality) imply for the systematic reflection of moral theology or Christian ethics? As noted before, moral theology must rely on distinctive Christian sources such as the gospel, Jesus, and the church. However, moral theology must also integrate the human ways of knowing and experiencing. This

approach was succinctly stated in the Pastoral Constitution on the Church in the Modern World, which, in the
preface to its discussion of the urgent moral questions to
be discussed in part two of the document, calls for a
consideration of these questions in the light of the gospel
and of human experience (par. 46).[30]

In the interest of furthering our dialogue some brief
comparisons can be made with positions which were
expressed during the Notre Dame conference. In general I
see my position as somewhere between the positions taken
by Stanley Hauerwas and Richard McCormick. My theological explanations indicate a broader and more universal understanding of church and of Christian ethics than I
detect in Hauerwas. On the issue of abortion I maintain,
apparently in disagreement with Hauerwas,[31] that Christians and all others in society must face the significant
question of when does human life begin. In arriving at
this important judgment Christians do not have any
moral insight which is not available to others. An
explicitly Christian value system (which again is not
exclusively Christian) certainly disposes one to give great
care to the poor and the little ones of this world, but we do
have to decide when truly individual human life begins
and when it ends.

I am not as certain about the exact nature of my
differences, if indeed there are any, with Richard McCormick on this question. According to McCormick the
confusion between paranetic and normative discourse is
probably the most common error in contemporary Christian ethics. I agree that specifically Christian motivation
for caring for the weak and defenseless can be called
paranesis. McCormick gives 1 Cor. 13:4–7 (love is patient,
etc.) as a clear example of paranesis. However, this
passage tells us many things about love as a Christian
value or disposition; there is true ethical content in this
description. Such content is not a concrete behavioral
norm, but it is ethical content and not simply paranesis or
exhortation. In addition, in speaking about the relationship between the Christian and the human, I maintain
that the human refers to the present historical reality of all

human beings called to share in God's saving love. As a practical consequence, I do not think that without that call the human person could accept and embrace the law of the cross, which admittedly is not a concrete behavioral norm. At times I have the impression that McCormick is working with a concept of the human which abstracts from the saving gift of God's love. If this is the case, there is a significant difference between us at least on the theoretical and theological level.

In addition to the consideration of the relationship of Christian morality and Christian ethics to human morality and human ethics, there arises the issue about how the Christian community should address the questions that are facing the larger pluralistic society in which we live.

In the past, Catholics generally addressed such questions on the basis of a natural law methodology, which by definition was supposed to be common to all human beings. The best examples of such an approach are the papal social encyclicals before the Second Vatican Council and, in the United States, the work of John Courtney Murray. However, the renewal of Catholic moral theology and the changing methodology, as illustrated in *Gaudium et spes*, have raised critical questions about such an approach. Many contemporaries also recognize that the language of natural law was not as universal as many of its adherents claimed it to be. The advantages of natural law as a universal language, as contrasted to the particular language of the Christian gospel, are not as clear-cut as once thought.

It is impossible to deal with the question in great depth. One should distingush between the way in which the church forms its own mind on these questions and the way in which it expresses its positions to the broader society. The Christian community of the church should make up its own mind on these issues on the basis of the methodology of moral theology as such—in the light of the gospel and human experience. In terms of expressing this position to others there can be room for both the gospel and human experience. Pragmatic concerns of effectiveness will be all important in making this choice. How-

ever, I would not want to eliminate apriori any reliance on
the gospel and on distinctively Christian warrants.

This chapter has addressed three significant methodological issues which will continue to be of great importance for moral theology—the nature of the discipline,
anthropology, and the multifaceted aspects of the important question about a distinctively Christian ethics and
morality.

NOTES

1. The substance of this chapter was originally presented as a
final summary paper at the conference on "Remembering and
Reforming: Towards a Constructive Christian Ethics," which
was sponsored by the Theology Department of the University of
Notre Dame. The papers of this conference will be published by
the University of Notre Dame.

2. See, for example, Bruce C. Birch and Larry L. Rasmussen,
Bible and Ethics in the Christian Life (Minneapolis, Minn.:
Augsburg, 1976).

3. Charles B. Moore, "This Is Medical Ethics?" *The Hastings
Center Report* 4, 5 (November 1974), 1-3.

4. Matthew Lamb, "The Theory-Praxis Relationship in
Contemporary Christian Theologies," *Proceedings of the Catholic Theological Society of America* 31 (1976), 149-178.

5. E.g., Enda McDonagh, *Doing the Truth: The Quest For
Moral Theology* (Notre Dame, Indiana: University of Notre
Dame Press, 1979), especially "Introduction: Theology as
Autobiography," pp. 1-13.

6. Häring has insisted on this dialogical character of the
Christian moral life from his earlist writings, but there have
been some significant developments from his *Law of Christ*, 3
vols. (Westminster, Ma.: Newman Press, 1961, 1963, 1966), first
published in Germany in 1954; and *Free and Faithful in Christ
I: General Moral Theology* (New York: Seabury Press, 1978).

7. In this connection one should note the failure of the
Constitution on the Sacred Liturgy of the Second Vatican

Council to underscore the important connection between liturgy and moral theology. In paragraph 16 the constitution urges those professors who teach disciplines other than liturgy, especially dogmatic theology, sacred scripture, and spiritual and pastoral theology, to set forth clearly the connection between their disciplines and the liturgy. No mention is made of moral theology.

8. Harvey G. Cox, *On Not Leaving It to the Snake* (New York: Macmillan, 1967), "Introduction" and throughout the book.

9. Joseph Fuchs, *Human Values and Christian Morality* (London and Dublin: Gill and Macmillan, 1970), pp. 92-111; Timothy E. O'Connell, *Principles for a Catholic Morality* (New York: Seabury, 1978), pp. 45-82.

10. In addition to Fuchs and O'Connell, see Häring, *Free and Faithful in Christ I*, pp. 164-222. The notes at the end of the chapter contain ample bibliographical references.

11. Stanley Hauerwas, *Character and the Christian Life: A Study in Theological Ethics* (San Antonio, Texas: Trinity University Press, 1975), pp. 179-228. Note that Hauerwas addresses the question of character and growth primarily from the theological perspective. His concept of the self as agent differs from the understanding of the person as a self-transcending subject.

12. Barnard Häring, "Conversion," in Ph. Delhaye et al., *Pastoral Treatment of Sin* (New York: Desclée, 1968), pp. 87-176. For Häring's latest discussion of the question, see *Free and Faithful in Christ I*, pp. 417-470.

13. Bernard J.F. Lonergan, "Theology in Its New Context," in *Theology of Renewal*, ed. L.K. Shook (New York: Herder and Herder, 1968), pp. 34-46; Lonergan, *Method in Theology* (New York: Herder and Herder, 1972), especially pp. 237-244. The importance of conversion in Lonergan's thought is indicated by the fact that in the index there are more references to conversion than to any other topic or person. For a well-edited book bringing together readings from many different perspectives on conversion, see Walter E. Conn, *Conversion: Perspectives on Personal and Social Transformation* (Staten Island, New York: Alba House, 1978).

14. Walter Eugene Conn, *Conscience: Development and Self-Transcendence* (Birmingham, AL: Religious Education Press, 1981).

15. André Guindon, "Moral Development: Form, Content and Self: A Critique of Kohlberg's Sequence," *Revue de l'Université d'Ottawa* 48 (1979), 232–263; Paul J. Philibert, "Conscience: Development Perspectives from Rogers and Kohlberg," *Horizons* 6 (1979), 1–25.

16. John Howard Yoder, *The Christian Witness to the State* (Newton, Kansas: Faith and Life Press, 1964); Yoder, *Karl Barth and the Problem of War* (New York and Nashville: Abingdon Press, 1970); Yoder, *The Politics of Jesus* (Grand Rapids, Michigan: William B. Eerdmans Publishing Co., 1972).

17. Stanley Hauerwas, *Vision and Virtue: Essays in Christian Ethical Reflection* (1974; Notre Dame, Indiana: University of Notre Dame Press, 1981), pp. 244, 245. These pages are cited by Malloy in his paper.

18. *Pacem in terris* and later documents of the universal church can conveniently be found in *The Gospel of Justice and Peace: Catholic Social Teaching Since Pope John*, ed. Joseph Gremillion (Maryknoll, New York: Orbis Press, 1976), pp. 201–203.

19. Ibid., pp. 243–335.

20. Daniel C. Maguire, *The Moral Choice* (Garden City, New York: Doubleday, 1978).

21. Hauerwas has occasionally dealt with specific moral decision making and even here insists on a different approach for the Christian. Stanley Hauerwas, "Theological Reflections on *In Vitro* Fertilization," in Ethics Advisory Board, Department of Health, Education and Welfare, *Appendix: HEW Support of Research Involving Human In Vitro Fertilization and Embryo Transfer*, May 4, 1979; Hauerwas, "Abortion: Why the Arguments Fail," *Hospital Progress* 61 (January 1980), 38–49.

22. Gremillion, *Gospel of Justice and Peace*, p. 514.

23. "Human Development and Christian Salvation," a statement issued by the International Theological Commission, *Origins* 7, 20 (November 3, 1977), 311.

24. Charles E. Curran, "Is There a Distinctively Christian Social Ethic?" in *Metropolis: Christian Presence and Responsibility*, ed., Philip D. Morris (Notre Dame, Indiana: Fides Publishers, 1970), pp. 92–120.

25. O'Connell, *Principles*, p. 40. "Thus, in a certain sense, moral theology is not theology at all. It is moral philosophy pursued by persons who are believers."

26. James J. Walter, "Christian Ethics: Distinctive and Specific," *American Ecclesiastical Review* 169 (1975), 470-489.

27 Norbert J. Rigali, "On Christian Ethics," *Chicago Studies* 10 (1971), 227-247.

28. These concepts were emphasized in the 1965 "Ariccia draft" and incorporated into the final document. See William J. Bergen, "The Evolution of the Pastoral Constitution on the Church in the Modern World: A Study in Moral Methodology," (S.T.D. diss., Catholic University of America, 1971).

29. Gremillion, *Gospel of Justic and Peace*, pp. 392-393.

30. Ibid., p. 282.

31. Hauerwas, "Abortion," 38-49.

PART THREE

Personal Ethics

5. A Theological Perspective on Aging

This chapter attempts to give a theological perspective on aging and the elderly. A few preliminary clarifications are in order.

Theology can be described as systematic reflection on human life and experience in the light of faith. Theological reflection does not pretend to have all the answers or to solve all the problems confronting humanity. Theology in fact must be in intimate contact and dialogue with human experience and with all that science and reason can tell us about the human. I theologize out of the Roman Catholic tradition, which has constantly emphasized that theological reflection involves both faith and reason and has gone so far as to assert that there cannot be a contradiction between faith and reason. Theology, therefore, cannot dispense with biology, sociology, psychology, gerontology medicine, and all the other sciences which tell us about the human. Theology is constantly learning from the human and the experience of the human in all its various dimensions.

Our title avoids any pretension at giving a complete theology of the aging, for our goal is much more modest— a theological perspective on aging and the elderly. This perspective will deal primarily with the question of the meaning and understanding of aging and not with programmatic or policy approaches. Theology itself should have something to contribute to the ongoing dialogue about programmatic and policy questions concerning the aging and elderly in our country, but still the primary

function of theology should be in terms of the more
ultimate questions of meaning. Even here in the question
of the meaning and significance of aging a theological
perspective recognizes the important contributions made
to the meaning of aging by the other human sciences and
must be in constant dialogue with them.

In many contemporary discussions about aging and the
elderly the meaning and significance of aging in the light
of faith-filled reflection are often not discussed. One can
readily understand the reason for such a gap. In our
pluralistic society there are many different faith perspectives as well as many different positions which claim to
exclude all faith presuppositions. The easiest way to solve
such a pluralism is to leave these ultimate questions of
faith and meaning to the individual and to the private
sphere, whereas the scientific, programmatic, and policy
aspects of these questions can be dealt with in public
dialogue. Unfortunately a dichotomy is thus set up, and
the questions of ultimate meaning tend to be ignored both
in themselves and in their important relationship to what
should be involved in the programmatic and policy
approaches to the aging.

Recently I viewed a proposed series of TV shows on
questions of bioethics. It was interesting to note the
tendency to stay away from questions of ultimate meaning, because these questions obviously involve a faith
perspective on which many people in our society differ.
Both theoretically and practically there are problems in
not addressing these questions of meaning as interpreted
by faith. Theoretical considerations remain incomplete
and even distorted when some important questions of
meaning are not discussed. From a practical perspective I
think most people in our society would admit that faith or
even lack of faith is a very significant aspect of their
understanding of human existence and especially of
human death. To pretend that this important aspect does
not exist or does not color the way in which people
actually think about death seems to distort the reality
itself. On this particular series of television programs all
other aspects of the question were mentioned and dis-

cussed—the biological, the sociological, the psychological, and in addition various programmatic and public
policy issues were raised. The ultimate question of
meaning was studiously avoided.[1]

One must appreciate the opposite danger. Religious
pluralism is a fact of life in our society. In many ways we
have suffered as a nation when one group tries to impose
its religious convictions upon others in public life. The
problem requires a balancing of our faith understanding
and our respect for the consciences of others and their
different faith. The easiest solution to the problem seems
to be the path of least resistence which is most often
taken—all such questions of ultimate meaning involving
faith are excluded from the public forum and public
debate. However, it is precisely such a solution which is
inadequate both on theoretical and on practical grounds.

The National Catholic School of Social Service of the
Catholic University of America as part of the celebration
of its sixtieth anniversary addressed the question of the
aging and elderly in our society. In my judgment precisely
such a school and such a forum should be the place in
which in a public manner the question about the ultimate
meaning and significance of aging, life, and death can and
should be raised.[2] In the context of this symposium my
considerations are based on a Roman Catholic theological
understanding. Obviously many people in our society
will bring to their consideration a different understanding
of aging and of life and death. Even so, those who do not
share this same faith vision may actually come to some of
the same conclusions which I will reach in this paper.
However, I make no apologies for my approach except to
note that it is obviously limited to those people who share
the same basic vision.

In discussions about the aging and the elderly there
always exists the danger of hubris, or pride, on the part of
those involved in the discussions. Too often the question
is explicitly or implicitly posed in terms of what society
can and should do for the aging and the elderly. The
presupposition is that the aging and the elderly have
nothing to say about us or about the worldview of our

society. In these days we recognize the danger that a majority group in society might very readily impose its self-understanding on others. One can think, for example, of the role of women in a male-dominated society. A Christian perspective reminds all of us of the need for conversion and the recognition of our own sinfulness so that we can be self-critical and enter into dialogue with others. There are important things that the aging and the elderly can say to the rest of us in our society.[3]

Aging and Death in the Light of the Paschal Mystery

One very common view of old age sees it in the light of a slope or peak view of human existence. There is a sharp upward movement representing childhood, youth, and adolescence, which then continues to develop at a lesser rate to a peak followed by a gradual decline, after which there is a sharp downward thrust of the curve in old age toward death. Such a vision of human existence tends to see the productive work which most adults do in our society as the most meaningful aspect of human existence. Childhood and adolescence are a preparation for work, and then retirement and old age indicate withdrawal from work and a downward curve in the meaning of human existence. In this paper such a view of the meaning of human existence will be challenged. Not only should we disagree with such an understanding of old age and the elderly, but we should also challenge its presuppositions about what is the meaning and dignity of human life.

The finality of death and its relationship to birth at the opposite end of the scale give credence to the slope view of human existence described above. To overturn such a view this paper will propose a different understanding of death.[4] The Christian concept of the paschal mystery sheds light on the meaning of death as well as the meaning of life for the Christian. The central mystery of Christianity is the dying and rising of the Lord, and through baptism Christians are initiated into the life of the risen Lord and share and participate in the paschal mystery.

Death in the Christian understanding has a number of different aspects.[5] Chapter three proposed a stance or perspective for Christian ethics which sees all reality in terms of the fivefold mysteries of creation, sin, incarnation, redemption, and resurrection destiny. In the light of this perspective three different aspects of death must be considered. First, biological death is the lot of all that exists. Death is inherently connected with our created, human, biological existence. In this sense death is a natural event. Second, death in the Christian understanding is ultimately connected with sin. According to St. Paul death came into the world through sin (Romans 5:12). In the book of Genesis, with its poignant meditation on the problem of evil, sin and death are closely related. Sin separates us from the giver of life. The natural consequence of sin is death. This is the ultimate explanation of the fact that those who sinned were no longer able to live with Yahweh in the peaceful relationship in the garden. If God did not intervene to save his people through Noah (which has become a symbol of salvation through the waters of baptism in the Christian tradition), sin would have come to its logical conclusion in the death and destruction of all that lives.[6] The New Testament sees the death of Jesus in terms of the power and even the triumph of sin and of the forces of darkness.

Third, death is also seen in the light of the resurrection and of the fullness of resurrection destiny. For Jesus death and sin were not the end. Through the resurrection which the scriptures attribute to the power of the Spirit (the one who gives life) Jesus triumphed over death itself. The resurrection transformed death into a saving mystery. One and the same reality which seemed to be the end and the triumph of sin was ultimately transformed into the victory of life itself. Thus there are three aspects of the meaning of death in the Christian understanding—death as natural and biological event, death as affected by sin, and death as transformed by the resurrection into the fullness of life.

The failure to consider all these aspects of death often results in a distortion. In the last few years the liturgical

emphasis in Roman Catholicism has focused on the
aspect of death as transformation through the power of
the resurrection. The vestments, the joyful songs, and the
hopeful refrains of the Mass of the Resurrection testify to
such an approach. While agreeing with the primacy of the
resurrecton motif, I am fearful that present Catholic
celebration and articulation do not give enough emphasis
to the aspect of death as affected by sin. Death is rightly
associated with loneliness, isolation, and loss. Death is
something over which we have no ultimate control.
Especially in the death of the young or death by accident
the brutal and harsh reality of death becomes even more
evident. The full reality of death as affected by sin should
not be too easily glossed over in the light of the gratuitous
grace of the resurrection. Yes, the resurrection transforms
the reality of death, but one must always experience the
sin-related aspect of death and all that is connected with
it.[7]

Our understanding of death as seen in the light of a
natural event infected by sin and transformed by the
resurrection raises further questions about the exact
relationship between life in this world and life after death.
The Christian belief calls for life after death, but what is
its relationship to life in this world? Is this relationship
one of continuity or discontinuity between this world and
the next? In more technical terms, is the paschal mystery
of death and resurrection to be interpreted in paradoxical
or in transformationalist terms? Arguments for discontinuity and a paradoxical understanding are based on the
apparent opposition between the symbols and explanations used to describe the paschal mystery in Jesus—life in
the midst of death, light in the midst of darkness, joy in
sorrow, and power in weakness. Death thus appears as a
complete break separating two different aspects of existence—earthly life which ends in death and the heavenly
life which begins anew. Pushed to its logical conclusions,
this view understands our present world and existence
primarily as a vale of tears marked above all by the
presence of sin, suffering, and death from which the
Christian is mercifully saved by the gracious intervention

of God, who after death brings the individual to the new life. Life in the world and the future life appear to be in a paradoxical or discontinuous relationship.

However, I would argue for more continuity between this world and the next, between life before death and life after death. In this view death for the Christian is seen more in transformational terms, with some continuity between this life and the next, although obviously there is not total continuity.[8]

An older, scholastic Catholic theology stressed more the aspect of continuity rather than total discontinuity. This theology viewed eternal life primarily in terms of immortality rather than in the more biblical concept of resurrection. Immortality is ultimately grounded in the spiritual nature of the human soul created by God, which even now is the form of our existence. Such a perspective emphasized continuity but neglected the importance of the material, the bodily, the worldly, and the social aspects of human existence and did not give enough importance to the concept of resurrection. Traditional scholastic theorizing about eternal life described it in terms of the beatific vision. The two highest faculties or powers of the human soul are intellect and will. The whole dynamism of human existence is grounded in the fact that our intellect and will are striving for the true and the good. Heaven or eternal life must involve fulfillment of the intellect and the will which alone can give perfect rest and peace—the intellect knows truth itself and the will loves the perfect good. Again, criticisms of this understanding are in order, but the basic thrust of the understanding argues for some continuity between this life and the next.[9]

The very words death and life seem to argue for discontinuity and a totally paradoxical relationship between this world and the next. However, our Christian understanding sees the paschal mystery of Jesus as paradigmatic of the whole of the Christian life and not only of Christian death. Through baptism the Christian first enters into the paschal mystery. Through baptism we die to sin and rise in the newness of the life of the risen Lord. The Christian even now in life shares in the first fruits of the resurrection. Thus, after death we share in the fullness of that which is now ours in its first fruits as the gift of the resurrected Lord to all who believe. Death for the Christian does not mark a total break with what has gone before, because one has already been sharing in the life of the risen Lord. Theology in the 1960s became too optimistic and saw too much continuity between this world and the next, between human progress and the coming of the kingdom. However, death for the individual Christian should be seen, not as the ending of life and the beginning of an entirely different reality, but rather as a transformation of our earthly existence into the fullness of the life of the risen Lord.

How does such an understanding correspond with human experience? As mentioned earlier, theology must always be in touch with human experience. Is there anything in human experience which would support (not prove) the transformationist understanding of death and the recognition of some continuity between this world and the next? A phenomenological view of human existence has been proposed which is in harmony with such a transformationist view.[10]

In human existence one can readily see two different curves—an upward curve and a downward curve. At first sight it might seem that such an understanding of these two curves would support the slope or peak theory—a curve which in the very beginning goes upward until it reaches a peak and then gradually descends until it suddenly cascades to its finality of old age and death.

There is no doubt that a downward curve is more evident and pronounced in older life, and death appears to be the ultimate fulfillment of this downward curve. Aging and old age bring with it a diminishment often accompanied by pain, suffering, loneliness, and isolation. The biological and physical aspects of human existence slow up and begin to diminish. The deterioration which started with glasses for the eyes, dentures for lost teeth, and hearing aids for deaf ears quickly seems to spread throughout the physical organism. Limbs shrivel, bones stiffen, arthritis inflames the joints. How sad it is at times to see old people who were so vibrant and full of energy now reduced to a wheel chair or totally confined to a bed. Those who during life ranged far and wide are now confined often within the limits of a room, a bed, or a chair. People who had social and professional responsibilities of great magnitude are now reduced to almost total dependence on others for anything they might want to do or even to fulfill their own basic needs. At times deterioration also affects the mental powers—memory goes, intellectual stimuli are lessened, and thought becomes confused. Advancing old age is often characterized by greater and greater passivity and dependence.

However, there is an upward curve about human existence that speaks of growth and development and is characterized by a growing self-encounter, a greater and deeper expansion of our relationships with other persons, and the growing encounter with our God. This upward curve can be seen in many aspects of our human existence. From earliest years the upward thrust entails a movement from dependence on others in a narrow environment to a greater independence and an overcoming of the limitations of time and space. Childhood and adolescence obviously mark such a growth toward a true independence (note that this is not to be understood in a selfish way) and at the same time to a greater widening of our horizons and relationships. This upward thrust continues through maturity, for here the individual both strives to become more and more the creative center of one's own existence and more deeply related to others in everwidening horizons and relationships. Through graceful maturity the individual comes to an evermore deepening self-encounter whereby one is less perturbed by the immediate happenings of existence and is able to be much less influenced by the changing circumstances of life. This is the ideal picture of the wise old person who, having seen the beauty of human existence and its degradations, having experienced the love of other human beings, and having known as well hatred and vengeance, now serenely and peacefully views human existence and strives for meaning and intelligibility. Now, less dependent than ever on the vicissitudes of time and space and purified in the struggle of human existence, the aging person comes to grips with oneself in an ever-deepening encounter and acceptance of who one is and how life should be lived. The upward curve also indicates growing and deeper relationships with others, as, through the direct experience of life and manifold vicarious experiences, the aging person overcomes the narrowness and confines of one's own historicity and tends to broaden and deepen relationships and horizons. In this process the believer also sees a growth in a relationship with God. Thus the ideal picture of the upward curve of human existence involves a richer encounter with ourselves, ever broadening and widening of our horizons and relationships with others, and a strengthening of our relationship with the source of all life itself.

How can old age and death be interpreted in the light of these theological and phenomenological considerations? The believing Christian sees death, not as the end, but as a way to the fullness of life. Death at first seems to be the triumph of the downward curve of existence, but the believer sees through death the ultimate triumph of the upward curve. Eternal life can be interpreted as the upward curve of human existence coming to the fullness of self-encounter, to the fullness of our relationships with our God. Thus death remains the ambivalent reality par excellence—apparently the end except for those who believe it is the entry into the fullness of life whereby the present is transformed and ultimately brought to its fullness.

Applications of the Theory

In the light of this understanding of the paradigm of the paschal mystery and of a transformationist interpretation of death a number of significant applications can be made to our appreciation of life in general and of old age in particular.

First, death is understood in the perspective of a crisis situation in which destructive and threatening forces are ultimately transformed. The crisis situation of death has great similarities with other growth and crisis situations in human existence in which the believer sees again the paschal mystery at work. In the crisis of early life the paradigm described above is quite evident. Take the child's first day in school. It is usually a traumatic experience—something new and threatening replacing the security and comfort of a former situation. No wonder that tears and tantrums so often mark that day. Growth demands a dying to the past so that one can go beyond it— but it is always a painful process. The essential ambiguity is that the type of existence which gave comfort and security now becomes narrow, confining, and limiting. Growth calls for us to pass beyond this stage so that we might enter into a deeper experience of life. But the pain of dying to the past and rising in the newness of life will always be there.

Christian marriage serves as another illustration. Marriage calls for the wife and husband to die to the past and to enter into the newness of life. We are reminded in the scriptures that for this reason they shall leave father and mother, brothers and sisters, and cling to one another as two in one flesh. Yet, joy and happiness abound at the celebration of marriage, but there also remain fears, insecurities, and even a sense of pain, loss, and separation. Death and the crisis of old age preceding it should be seen in the same light. Here, too, it is necessary to pass beyond the limits of old age that prevent further self-development. Ultimately the crisis of death involves dying in order that the fullness of life might come. We see only one side of the crisis of death with our eyes, but our hearts through faith and hope rely on a deeper meaning of transformation that will take place and even now is at work. The crisis of death involving dying and rising is thus related to other crises in our lives.

Such a view of human existence and growth in human existence coheres with an understanding of life as a

pilgrimage. Christian anthropology today often refers to
our human existence as a pilgrimage in which we are
called to continual conversion.[11] As pilgrims we are
constantly on the road—change and growth always
characterize our lives, and the challenge is to make these
changes into true growth. Growth and development are
not just physical and biological. Too often we tend to
think of growth only in these very visible and quantifiable
ways. The peak model of human development shares this
basic narrowness of perspective. Growth calls above all for
a greater encounter with one's self, with others, with all of
creation, and with God. Too often we fail to realize what
constitutes true growth and thereby falsify our understanding of life, of old age, and of dying itself. A world
that has begun to listen to the message that small is
beautiful should also be ready to abandon our more
quantifiable and less personal criteria of what truly
constitutes human growth and development.

A second corollary based on the importance of the
paschal mystery as an interpretation of Christian death,
old age, and life concerns the active aspect of death and of
old age. The literature generally describes old age and
death in terms of passivity. Death readily fits into the
category. We have no control over our death. In a sense it
comes from outside and thrusts itself upon us. Infirmity
and death are seldom willed or intended by ourselves but
come despite our best efforts. The same can be said of old
age. But such a judgment of death and of old age is
distorted. Death and old age also involve a very active
aspect which must be more recognized and acknowledged
if we are to come to a better understanding of their
meaning.

Look again at the death and resurrection of Jesus. Death
is forced on Jesus from the outside. He is led to death as a
sheep to the slaughter. The enemies of Jesus described
under the theological symbols of death and sin are the
active elements in the drama of the crucifixion. Jesus is
passively dragged from here to there and finally nailed to
the cross on which he died. But Jesus through the loving
gift of himself and the loving acceptance of his death has

actively transformed death into a saving mystery. Death has been changed through the power of his love into the resurrection and the fullness of life.

Many contemporary theologians likewise maintain that death for the Christian involves a very decisive and creative act and is not just something one passively endures from the outside. In the moment of death the Christian affirms one's deepest self-encounter and at the same time one's relationship with God and with all others. Once the restrictions and confining realities of our aging earthly existence are dissolved, the Christian can then fully affirm oneself in loving relationship with God, others, and the self. In death the limitations of the present fade away, and the person can now fully affirm oneself in terms of these multiple relationships.[12] Even from the psychological perspective Kübler-Ross points out the final reaction to death is acceptance—but here, too, there is an active element present and not a mere receptivity.[13] For the Christian it is a hope-filled acceptance in the light of seeing death as a way to eternal life through transformation.

In the same sense old age calls for activity—but activity properly understood. Too often activity is described in terms of external goods and technological productivity. Obviously old age in this sense is less productive and less active. However, look at the works of art, music, and literature that have been done by people in old age. At the very least such a consideration reminds us that activity and productivity should not be confined merely to material things and a technological understanding of human existence.

The challenge of old age is to be truly active—in the sense of accepting old age, appropriating it, giving it meaning, and integrating it into oneself as a person. Some philosophers characterize the human person as a meaning giver. This is the active aspect of personal development for all of us—to give meaning to our existence and to incorporate all the realities of life into the intregrated whole of the person. Yes, in a technological sense we produce less in old age: we do less in terms of the material and physical; but we are called upon to be active, to give meaning and intelligibility to our lives. The old and the old-old should truly be active in the most personal sense of being active—giving meaning and intelligibility to their lives. For the Christian the meaning comes in terms of the living out of the paschal mystery by which we come to know and experience the Lord in the fellowship of his suffering and in the power of his resurrection.[14]

Our human experience seems to support the above analysis. Look at those who in our judgment have aged successfully—and not just those who are in good physical shape but even those who have suffered handicaps and debilities. These are the people who have actively given meaning to their life and integrated all aspects of their existence into their person. We all admire the truly beautiful person who cheerfully bears witness to what it means to be human. A recognition of the true activity of all life and of old age belies the often-accepted notion of old age as passive. The old face the crisis and challenge of giving meaning to their existence. A more scientific rendering of the psychology of human existence also seems to corroborate the active aspects of old age.[15] Erikson has proposed a theory of ego development in which the stage of aging is characterized by what he called integrity. Integrity involves an acceptance of one's own and only life and a detached and yet active concern with life itself.[16]

As a third corollary, the ways in which this understanding of old age calls into question some common assumptions in our society can be discussed. Too often society attributes value and dignity to persons in terms of what they do, make, or accomplish. The person becomes identified with one's job. However, the Christian vision sees dignity and worth primarily in terms of the fact that life is a gift of the gracious God. Such an understanding of the value of human life not only calls into question many of the assumptions of our society but also furnishes a very solid basis for defending the basic equality of all human lives. A false quietism would deny any value to human actions and efforts, but the ultimate reason for human dignity does not rest on our works or our accomplishments. The biblical emphasis on the importance of the needs of the neighbor underscores the danger of judging others and ranking them of the basis of what they do.

Throughout this chapter a technological view of human meaning and existence has been challenged. Chapter seven will discuss the relationship between the technological and the human in greater detail. There is a place for technology in human development, but the human can never be reduced merely to the technological.[17] Too often our society is in danger of making that reductionism. Intimately connected with such a view is the insistence on technologically productive work as the ultimate meaning of human existence. As a result, we might reexamine our whole understanding of work and how it fits into the meaning of the human. Already some older patterns are changing because education is proposed as a lifelong process and not merely as a preparation for one's productive years. True, much of the need for continuing education is to keep abreast of modern technological developments, but some also indicates a recognition that there is more to life than material productivity.

The insistence on the fact that old age is characterized not by passivity but by truly human action also serves to correct many of our notions about what is human activity. The cult of youth and the emphasis on consumption in our society are also called into question by the understanding of old age and human activity proposed here.

The mutual relationship between the aging and others in society also stresses the social fabric of our existence and goes against the individualism which so often characterizes our society. Yes, in many ways the aging are in need of the help of others in society, but the relationship with the aging is more than a one-way street. This recognition of our mutual dependence and relationship would mean that the aging remain an integral part of society. Often the aging and the elderly have been segregated from society and isolated from others.

In conclusion, the limited aspect of this study must be recognized. The purpose has been narrowed to the question of the meaning of aging and old age for the Christian believer in the Catholic tradition. Any such presentation by its very nature tends to be abstract and idealistic. However, an attempt was made not to pass over the sufferings, diminishments, and problems that some people will encounter in old age. Realism recognizes that many people fail to give a meaning to their aging and do not age gracefuly. These failures together with all the sufferings of old age, as well as the failures and suffering of all life, are also seen in the light of the paschal mystery.

There is a danger that faith will be seen as an easy solution to the hard problems of life, aging, and dying. Here it is necessary to point out that faith in the paschal mystery does not protect one from the sorrows and sufferings of the cross, nor does such faith provide a cheap or easy victory. The pilgrimage character of Christian existence, together with the recognition of our apprehension of both the presence and the absence of God, has occasioned much writing in recent years about the crisis of faith both in general and in various times of development, especially in youth. Undoubtedly there also exists a crisis of faith for many in old age. The church itself is now recognizing more the importance of its role in ministering to the aging and the elderly.[18] As a result we hopefully will see some interdisciplinary studies about faith and even the problems and crisis of faith in the aging and the elderly.

What has been proposed here remains abstract and general. Every person must give meaning to one's life and aging in the context of the unique individuality that is the human person. Aging will have different effects on different people. Think of the differences in terms of health, wealth, familial, and social relationships; nevertheless, all must draw on faith and give meaning to their own aging. The understanding of aging and death proposed here should have some influence on the way in which Christian individuals appropriate and give meaning to their aging.

NOTES

1. For a negative critique of theological bioethics for failing to bring out the explicit faith dimensions of reality, see James M. Gustafson, "Theology Confronts Technology and the Life Sciences," *Commonweal* 105 (June 16, 1978), 386-392.

2. Mention should be made of other symposia which have tried to give importance to faith and theological perspectives. One of a continual series of Pastoral Psychology Institutes at Fordham University discussed the question of aging, and its proceedings have been published: *Aging: Its Challenge to the Individual and to Society,* ed. William C. Bier (New York: Fordham University Press, 1974). The National Retired Teachers Association and the American Association of Retired Persons sponsored a Conference on the Theology of Aging in the spring of 1974 whose proceedings were published in *Pastoral Psychology* 24 (Winter 1975), 93-176.

3. For a provocative statement of such an attitude, although the development of the main idea is somewhat disappointing, see Peter Naus, "The Elderly as Prophets," *Hospital Progress* 59 (May 1978), 66-68.

4. Other approaches have been employed by theologians to dispute the peak or slope view of human existence. Paul W. Preyser, "Aging: Downward, Upward or Forward?" *Pastoral Psychology* 24 (1975), 102-118, explicitly rejects "the peak-slope illusion." Henri J.M. Nouwen and Walter J. Gaffney, *Aging* (Garden City, New York: Doubleday, 1974), employ the "wagon wheel" model. David Tracy, "Eschatological Perspectives on Aging," *Pastoral Psychology* 24 (1975), 119-134, interprets aging in the light of an eschatological perspective calling for the acceptance of past, present, and future modalities of time.

5. My discussion on death is heavily influenced by the following three books: Ladislaus Boros, *The Mystery of Death* (New York: Herder and Herder, 1965); Karl Rahner, *On the Theology of Death* (New York: Herder and Herder, 1961); Roger Troisfontaines, *I Do Not Die* (New York: Desclée, 1963).

6. This concept of the Noachic covenant restraining the destructive power of sin is well developed in Lutheran theology. See Helmut Thielicke, *Theological Ethics I: Foundations* (Philadelphia: Fortress Press, 1966), pp. 439ff and passim.

7. Leo J. O'Donovan, "The Prospect of Death," in *Aging: Its Challenge to the Individual and to Society*, ed. William C. Bier, pp. 212-224. O'Donovan insists on not oversimplying death by recognizing the aspects of fear, loneliness, and suffering as well as trust, communion, and redemption.

8. For a more complete development of a transformational understanding of the paschal mystery, contrasting it both in theory and in practice with a paradoxical understanding, see my "Crisis of Spirituality in Priestly Ministry," *American Ecclesiastical Review* 166 (1972), 94-111, 157-173.

9. For a contemporary insistence on immortality and its importance for Christian ethics in this present world, see Marjorie Reiley Maguire, "Ethics and Immortality," *The American Society of Christian Ethics 1978: Selected Papers from the Nineteenth Annual Meeting*, ed. Max L. Stackhouse (Waterloo, Ontario, Canada: Council on the Study of Religion, 1978), pp. 42-61.

10. The authors mentioned in note 5 propose such a phenomenological view.

11. Conversion has become an important theme in contemporary theology. See *Conversion: Perspectives on Personal and Social Transformation*, ed. Walter E. Conn (Staten Island, New York: Alba House, 1978).

12. Some theologians are fearful of the concept of a final option at the moment of death, because it gives decisive importance to an act which does not take place in this world. See Gisbert Greshake, "Tod und Auferstehung: Alte Probleme neu überdacht," *Bibel und Kirche* 32 (1977), 2-11. However, one can avoid this problem by insisting on the continuity between that act and the whole life of the person in this world. For further objections to the theory, see Bruno Schüller, "Todsürde— Sünde zum Tod?" *Theologie und Philosophie* 42 (1967), 321-340.

13. Elizabeth Kübler-Ross, *On Death and Dying* (New York: Macmillan, 1970).

14. Edward Fischer has attempted to give meaning to old age by seeing it in terms of worship. See Edward Fischer, "Aging as Worship," *Worship* 52 (March 1978), 98-108.

15. For an explanation of a parish program for the aging based on a developmental theory of aging with a truly active role

for the aging, see M. Vincentia Joseph, "The Parish and Ministry to the Aging," *The Living Light* 14 (1977), 69-83.

16. For an exposition and application of Erikson's theory of development to the aging, see Don S. Browning, "Preface to a Practical Theology of Aging," *Pastoral Psychology* 24 (1975), 151-167.

17. Drew Christiansen makes an interesting distinction between neonaturalism and technological humanism. I agree with the basic idea, but the distinction should never become a total dichotomy. Drew Christiansen, "Ethical Implications in Aging," *Encyclopedia of Bioethics* I, ed. Warren T. Reich (New York: The Free Press, 1978), pp. 63, 64.

18. Alfons Deeken, *Growing Old, and How to Cope with It* (New York: Paulist Press, 1972); Leonard J. Rizzo, "Participatory Catechesis and the Elderly," *The Living Light* 12 (1975), 100-103; Sara and Richard Reichert, *In Wisdom and the Spirit: A Religious Education Program for Those Over Sixty-Five* (New York: Paulist Press, 1976). In 1976 the Roman Catholic bishops of the United States issued a statement entitled "Society and the Aged: Towards Reconciliation." The text is found in *Origins: N.C. Documentary Service* (May 20, 1976), 758-761.

6. *In Vitro* Fertilization and Embryo Transfer

This chapter will examine the ethical aspects of *in vitro* fertilization and embryo transfer from the perspective of Roman Catholic moral theology. A preliminary consideration will briefly explain the nature of moral theology and its relationship to other disciplines.

Introduction: Moral Theology

Moral theology in a systematic and thematic way studies human behavior and acts from the perspective of the Roman Catholic faith understanding. There are three distinguishing characteristics of moral theology—a faith perspective and its implications, the use of reason, and the teaching role of the church community.

All religious ethics share a dependence on a faith perspective and thus are differentiated from all purely philosophical or rational ethics. Roman Catholic moral theology with its proper faith perspective shares much in common with Jewish ethics and especially with Protestant ethics. The reality of faith shapes the experience of the individual believer, establishes the believing community of the church, and finds a privileged written source in the revealed scriptures.

Second, moral theology accepts the importance of human reason and its role as a source of ethical wisdom and knowledge for Christians and for all others. The Catholic tradition has traditionally upheld the principle that faith and reason can never contradict one another. Thomas Aquinas, the most significant figure in the Catholic theological tradition, exemplifies this acceptance of human reason, since he employed the thought of the pagan philosopher Aristotle to understand and express better the Christian faith itself. Catholic moral theology has traditionally given heavy emphasis to the natural law approach in studying human actions. The natural law is aptly described as human reason directing human beings to their ultimate end in accord with their human nature. Through human reason we share and participate in the reasonable plan of God for the world.[1]

There are many significant theoretical questions about the relationship between faith and reason in moral theology. However, the history of Catholic moral theology indicates that for the most part human reason has been the primary basis for the teaching proposed on medical ethics and on specific moral issues such as *in vitro* fertilization or artificial insemination.[2] Chapter four explained my agreement with the position proposed by a good number of contemporary Catholic moral theologians that there is no specifically unique content to Christian morality which is not available to the experience of all human beings existing in our world.[3]

The reliance on human reason in solving specific ethical questions is well illustrated in the discussion of artificial insemination by Pope Pius XII in 1949 and in his subsequent references to this question and to *in vitro* fertilization.[4] The pope's ethical teaching is grounded in human reason and human nature, which are by definition distinct from faith and available to all human beings.

Appeals to faith can and do shape the general approaches and perspectives which one brings to a particular question. Some perspectives might be incompatible with a faith vision. A Christian faith vision would be wary of any utopian scheme for the ultimate perfection of the human race through science or technology. The Christian vision recognizes the specifically human aspects existing in the innermost depths of the human person—the basic realities of freedom, self-determination, grace, and sin.

Finitude, evil, and death will always characterize human existence, but at the same time the Christian who shares now in the new life of the resurrection should try to overcome sin. However, the fullness of the kingdom will never exist in this world but will always be God's gracious gift at the end of time.

Different emphases within the Christian perspective might result in different attitudes. Christian anthropology allows for different interpretations. Paul Ramsey, a Methodist ethicist, sees in the attempt of human beings to control their human future through genetic manipulation and the alteration of human parenthood the basic sin of pride, or *hubris*—the temptation to play God and to deny our creatureliness.[5] On the other hand Harvey Cox maintains that the great sin of human beings is not pride but sloth—the refusal to take responsibility for our future life.[6] Likewise, Christian eschatology allows for different perspectives. Ramsey stresses discontinuity between this world and the next and hence is somewhat pessimistic about progress and development in human life. Others, such as Harvey Cox in his earlier writings, see a greater continuity between this world and the next so that they are more optimistic about what human beings can do in the world. Joseph Fletcher, in his writings on bioethics, implicitly accepts an anthropology and eschatology similar to that proposed by Cox.[7] These positions are examined at greater length and criticized in the next chapter.

A third characteristic of Catholic moral theology is the role of the church. In agreement with other Christian ethics, Catholic moral theology acknowledges a role for the church as a moral teacher. The distinctively unique Catholic understanding of the church recognizes a special teaching role belonging to the hierarchical magisterium (the teaching office of popes and bishops) in the church. Of special importance for this paper is the papal teaching office. The infallible teaching office is distinguished from the authoritative, authentic noninfallible teaching office. The latter teaching office is generally exercised by the pope in encyclicals written to the bishops of the church and to all Catholics, in papal allocutions and addresses to more limited audiences, and in the decrees of the Roman congregations which carry out the work of the church. Catholic theologians generally agree that on specific moral questions treated in encyclicals, and especially in the less authoritative form of papal allocutions, the authoritative, authentic noninfallible papal teaching office is usually being exercised.[8] A few decades ago it was widely held that if the pope goes out of his way to speak on a controverted subject, it is no longer a matter of free debate among Catholic theologians.[9]

This understanding of the response to the papal teaching office has recently been challenged. Chapter one discussed in detail the role of theology in the church. Many Roman Catholic theologians today maintain that dissent from noninfallible papal teaching is a possible option for Catholic theologians and faithful alike. In fact, the possibility of such dissent is proposed as totally in keeping with the traditional self-understanding of the Roman Catholic Church even though it was not popularly recognized.[10] Whether or not dissent is allowed on specific issues depends on the particular case, and here there is much discussion. Recall the controversies within the Roman Catholic Church about artificial contraception for married couples. In my judgment the Catholic moral theologian must always acknowledge the unique hierarchical teaching office and respect its teaching but at times can and even should dissent from its teaching.

The discipline of moral theology must give attention to these three aspects or sources of moral theology—faith, reason, and the teaching of the church. Moral theology is a discipline with a long history, so that anyone who is working in this discipline must be familiar with that historical development but at the same time be in constant dialogue with those other religious ethics with which so much is shared and also with contemporary philosophical and scientific thought.

The body of this paper will now examine the question of *in vitro* fertilization and embryo transfer from the perspective of Roman Catholic moral theology.[11] The first section addresses ethical questions and issues which have been in the past the subject of much discussion by theologians and are also connected with the ethical evaluation of this new reproductive technology. The second section will consider the specific question of *in vitro* fertilization and embryo transfer.

I. Ethical Issues Previously Discussed

This section will discuss questions that have previously been treated by theologians apart from the specific topic of this paper but which are also involved in evaluating embryo culture and transfer. The following major issues will be identified and treated: anthropological presuppositions; obtaining sperm and oocytes; the meaning of human parenthood; the beginning of truly human life.

Anthropological presuppositions

Anthropological presuppositions can be reduced to the attitudes toward human existence, progress in human history, and technology. All who discuss specific ethical questions have such attitudes and presuppositions even if they are not explicitly articulated. These attitudes may be derived from a faith vision or they may be grounded in other sources. For the moral theologian these attitudes are greatly influenced by a faith perspective. There can be optimistic or pessimistic views of human persons, progressive or despairing views of human progress in history, positive and negative attitudes to technology. The following paragraphs will briefly summarize the position which will be developed in the next chapter.

My theological perspective or stance views human existence in terms of the fivefold Christian mysteries of creation, sin, incarnation, redemption, and resurrection destiny. Obviously such a horizon eliminates one-sided approaches to these questions. Human beings are created good, share even now in the power of the risen Lord, and look forward to the fullness of eternal life. However, human finitude will always exist; sin still affects the hearts of human beings and the structures of social existence, and the future of the fullness of life always lies beyond us. In this perspective there exists a possibility for some truly human progress despite setbacks and the ever-present threats, but any naively optimistic or progressive understanding of human progress is denied.

From a more philosophical perspective, Thomas Aquinas, the most significant Roman Catholic theologian, anticipated many moderns by basing his ethics on the human being who is an image of God precisely insofar as being endowed with intellect, free will, and the power of self-determination.[12] However, human beings exist as corporeal persons in time and space with other human beings and have obligations and rights in reference to others; they are more than merely freedom events. One practical conclusion is that freedom is not the only ethical consideration, because other elements (e.g., justice) might enter into consideration. For example, some human experimentations will be morally wrong even though all the parties involved freely consent to them.

Technology will always be at the service of the human, but the human includes much more than just the scientific or the technological. The ecology question reminds us that technological progress and human progress are not the same. Sometimes in the name of the human it is necessary to say no to what one type of technology or one science can do.

Obtaining sperm and oocytes

The Roman Catholic papal magisterium has been opposed to artificial insemination (AIH) because masturbation cannot be used to obtain sperm. As early as 1897 the Congregation of the Holy Office decreed that artificial insemination was illicit.[13] In the light of previous and subsequent theological positions the decree was interpreted to condemn artificial insemination precisely because the seed was obtained by means of masturbation. Before that decree was issued, two moral theologians (Palmieri and Berardi) indicated that perhaps masturba-

tion in the case of artificial insemination would not be
wrong because the seminal ejaculation was directed to the
fecundation of the ovum. After the decree of 1897 both
authors retracted their position.

In 1919 Arthur Vermeersch proposed that artificial
insemination is not morally wrong if the semen is not
obtained by means of masturbation. He suggested the
puncturing of the epididimus or anal friction or massage.
Many Catholic theologians writing before 1949 agreed
with this position, thereby indicating that the reason for
the condemnation of artificial insemination in 1897 was
due to the fact that the semen was obtained through
masturbation.[14] Masturbation as a means of obtaining
semen for curing infertility or for seminal analysis was
condemned by the Holy Office in 1929[15] and again by
Pope Pius XII in 1956.[16] In 1949 in his first address on
artificial insemination Pope Pius XII also condemned
masturbation and all acts contrary to nature as means of
obtaining semen.

The official papal teaching and the theologians appeal
to human reason and the natural law to justify the
condemnation of masturbation as a way of obtaining
semen either for artificial insemination or for seminal
analysis. The sexual faculty has a twofold purpose—
procreation and love union. Every sexual actuation must
be an act which is open to procreation and expressive of
love. The act of masturbation is always wrong because it is
neither open to procreation nor expressive of love. No
good end or purpose can ever justify an act which is
always and everywhere wrong. One could for a sufficient
reason licitly take semen from the male, but not by means
of sexual actuation.[17]

Today the majority of Roman Catholic theologians
writing on the subject reject such reasoning and its
conclusion. Masturbation is not always and intrinsically
wrong. These theologians disagree with the act-analysis
of the older approach and with the underlying concept of
intrinsically evil actions when the action is defined in
terms of the physical structure of the act itself. Although
there are different ways of explaining a newer approach,

opponents of the older position agree that the problem is one of physicalism—identifying the human moral act with the physical structure of the act. The intentionality and purpose also codetermine the moral meaning of the act. The procuring of semen for semen analysis or for AIH is judged not to be morally wrong.[18]

Such discussions also remind us that the obtaining of sperm and oocytes can involve ethical issues. Today there are risks taken by the would-be mother involved in hormonal treatments to induce superovulation, in the process of removing oocytes by laparoscopy, in transferring the embryo, and in further monitoring. From an ethical perspective these risks are comparatively slight and can be justified by other values and reasons.

Nature of human parenthood

In vitro fertilization involves a new process of human parenthood which raises the question about what is ethically normative in terms of human parenthood. Various aspects of the question have been considered in connection with artificial insemination with the husband's seed and also with a donor's seed. *In vitro* fertilization now allows for fertilization to occur outside the woman and offers the opportunity for women with problems such as occluded fallopian tubes to conceive in an artificial way and have a child of their own.

The first consideration will involve artificial insemination with the husband's sperm (AIH). In this case the so-called natural process of the ejaculation of male seed in the vagina of the female does not take place, but the husband's seed is artificially inseminated. The morality of this procedure (as distinct from the question of how the semen is obtained) was frequently discussed by Catholic moral theologians in the twentieth century. The opinion affirming the moral acceptance of AIH, provided the sperm was obtained without sexual actuation, was proposed by Arthur Vermeersch and then explained by Gerald Kelly.[19] Husband and wife have a right to propagate by any means which is not in itself evil. Just as every

human being has a natural right to preserve one's life and
can use artificial means to do so when the normal means
are not helpful or available, so the married couple, when
unable to generate by the normal means of marital
intercourse, may use artificial means provided they are not
sinful. The assumption in such reasoning is that artificial
insemination itself is not a sinful means. Theologians
were quite divided on this issue.[20]

This debate among Roman Catholic theologians came
to an end after Pope Pius XII's address to the Fourth
International Congress of Catholic Doctors on September
29, 1949. The pertinent part of the papal allocution
follows:

> Although one may not *a priori* exclude new methods for the
> sole reason that they are new, nevertheless, as regards artificial
> insemination, there is not only reason for extreme reserve, but
> it must be entirely rejected. To say this is not necessarily to
> proscribe the use of certain artificial means designed only to
> facilitate the natural act or to enable that act, performed in a
> normal manner, to attain its end.
>
> We must never forget this: It is only the procreation of new
> life according to the will and plan of the Creator which brings
> with it—to an astonishing degree of perfection—the realiza-
> tion of the desired ends. This is, at the same time, in harmony
> with the dignity of the marriage partners, with their bodily
> and spiritual nature, and with the normal and happy
> development of the child.[21]

In 1951 Pius XII again broached this topic and clarified
in greater detail the meaning of the marital act:

> In its natural structure the conjugal act is a personal action, a
> simultaneous and immediate cooperation on the part of the
> husband and wife which by the very nature of the agents and
> the propriety of the act is the expression of the mutual gift
> which according to Holy Scripture brings about union 'in
> one flesh only.' There is something much more than the
> union of two germ cells which may be brought about even
> artificially, without the natural action of husband and wife.
> The conjugal act ordained and willed by nature is a personal
> act of cooperation, the right to which husband and wife give
> each other when they marry.[22]

Moral theologians then attempted to state systematically and coherently the Catholic position on the nature of the marital act in the light of generally accepted theories and of these addresses of Pius XII. Sexual actuation which is in accord with the plan of God must be both open to procreation and expressive of love union. This is the nature of the sexual actuation which human beings must always observe. According to Ford and Kelly (recall that Kelly himself had previously favored AIH):

> For Pius XII seems to be saying that just as it is wrong to violate the natural design by excluding the basic procreativity of the act from the conjugal embrace (by contraception), so also it is wrong to violate the natural design by excluding the conjugal embrace, that is, the personal self-donation of the partners, from the procreative activity (by artificial insemination). Artificial insemination is condemned precisely because it separates procreation from the personal act of loving self-surrender. In other words the marriage act has a natural design as an act of conjugal love too.[23]

Often the official hierarchical teaching in the Roman Catholic Church has not been properly understood, especially in terms of its condemnation of artificial contraception. The official teaching is not pronatalist at any cost, as the condemnation of AIH testifies. The ultimate reason for the condemnation of both contraception and of AIH rests on an analysis of the sexual act itself. Sexuality has a twofold purpose—procreation and love union. Every sexual actuation must be both open to procreation and expressive of love. This analysis of the act and its God-given design provides the basis for the condemnation of artificial contraception and of AIH (as well as of masturbation). Logically, those who disagree with the official hierarchical teaching on contraception should also disagree with the condemnation of AIH, for both condemnations rest on the same act analysis. As a matter of fact, many Roman Catholic theologians today do not accept this analysis of the physical act and are in favor of contraception and AIH when there are sufficient reasons. To my knowledge, no contemporary Catholic theologian who has accepted artificial contraception has condemned AIH.

Sexual actuation does not always and everywhere by its very nature have to be both open to procreation and expressive of love union. Love union and procreation are united not in the act but rather in the marriage relationship and in the partners. Consequently, with many other Catholic theolgians I accept the morality of AIH.[24] In the contemporary literature outside Catholic moral theology it seems there have been no major attempts to prove that AIH is wrong.

In his address of September 29, 1949, Pope Pius XII condemned artificial insemination with donor sperm (AID) both outside and within marriage. The fundamental reason excluding AID is that the procreation of new life must be the fruit of the marriage and of the marriage partners. This is the primary reason against AID proposed by most Catholic theologians and by many others. Pope Pius XII phrased the objection primarily in terms of the rights of the spouses who alone have an exclusive, nontransferable, and inalienable right over their bodies for the purpose of generating new life.[25]

Those who reject AIH maintain that the act of sexual intercourse must be both open to procreation and expressive of love. Those opposed to AID argue that procreation and love union must always be united in the two persons who covenant their lives to one another in marriage. The child must be the fruit of their love and the fruit of their bodies. The inability of one of the partners to generate offspring is part of the "worse" of the marriage promises which the couple make to one another. The two have made a covenant to share their love and their life. To bring in an oocyte or a sperm from outside the covenant relationship violates the very meaning of this relationship.

Other arguments proposed against AID are based on the consequences that might come from such a procedure. AID might harm the future psychic development of the child-to-be. AID could cause psychic difficulties for the male who is unable to have a child of his own and could thereby threaten even the marriage itself. In addition, other undesirable consequences are the buying and selling of sperm and the depersonalization of the procreation of offspring.

In general I give great weight to the argument from the meaning of the marriage convenant and from the fact that the child is the fruit of the love and the bodies of husband and wife. However, I do not believe that these reasons constitute an absolute prohibition against AID. There are strong reasons to counsel against an easy acceptance of AID. Likewise, the other reasons proposed against it deserve serious consideration and are factors that cannot be readily passed over. In my judgment adoption is to be preferred. However, I cannot exclude the possibility that AID could be a morally good choice in some circumstances despite serious problems that are present. Ways could be developed of preventing some possible abuses. It would not be necessary to buy and sell sperm. In one clinic in France the sperm is freely donated by a married man who together with his wife consents to do this. In this way a personal aspect is maintained, and any grossness involved in selling sperm is avoided.[26]

It should be pointed out that the majority of Roman Catholic theologians condemn AID as morally wrong. Many who morally accept AIH do not allow AID.[27] Karl Rahner, who allows experimentation on *in vitro* fertilization, does not accept AID.[28] Debate also continues among other Christian ethicists and philosophers.[29]

AID outside marriage presents a different perspective, especially in the light of the Judaeo-Christian tradition which sees childbearing and rearing within the context of marriage. For this reason and all that lies behind it AID outside marriage is morally unacceptable. Further questions involving procreation and the meaning of parenthood will be discussed in later sections.

The beginning of human life

The beginning of truly human life looms large in any discussion of *in vitro* fertilization and embryo transfer. What is it that is present in the preimplantation embryo? In these discussions I avoid the term person and speak of

truly individual human life as that life which deserves the
same value, rights, and protection due the human person
as such.

In the context of the debate over abortion there have
been many articles and books written on the question of
the beginning of truly human life and the criteria or
methodological approaches to be employed in determining when truly human life begins. The papal and
hierarchical magisteria of the Roman Catholic Church
have shown complete unanimity even in recent years in
maintaining that from the moment of conception the
fetus is to be treated as truly human life. However, the
hierarchical magisterium still recognizes that theoretical
doubt about the beginning of human life can exist, but in
practice one must act as if truly human life is present from
the moment of conception.[30]

In the contemporary ethical writing on this topic I
discern four different types of criteria for deciding when
truly individual human life begins.[31] The individual-
biological criterion judges the existence of truly human
life in terms of some physical, biological, or genetic aspect
of the individual being. A relational criterion maintains
that truly human life begins once there is an established
human relationship between parents and fetus. A multiple criterion approach includes biological, psychological, and cultural factors with a developing value attached
to the fetus as all these factors are more present. A
conferred-rights criterion recognizes difficulties with the
metaphysical basis of the other proposals and affirms that
rights are conferred by those people who contract to make
up the society.

In evaluating these criteria and/or conclusions I begin
with the presupposition that almost all would accept that
infanticide is wrong. As a result, one must propose a
criterion for the beginning of truly individual human life
which can never be used to justify infanticide.

I reject the conferred-rights approach because it does
not go to the heart of the matter. Why should rights be
conferred on the fetus in the first place? In addition, my
philosophy of rights sees these as inalienable rights of the

human being and not something conferred by others. The relational criterion, if it is to be based on *human* relations as constituting the beginning of truly human life, would not be present until well after birth. Human relations involve some type of reciprocity. A multiple approach stresses the need for psychological and cultural factors as well as biological, but in my judgment there is much more psychological and cultural development which takes place after birth than takes place before birth. I employ the individual-biological criterion. In a sense this is the same general criterion used in our determination of human death. Whether the test for death be cessation of heartbeat, of breathing, or of electrical brain activity, these are all criteria of the individual-biological order.

Within this criterion I maintain that truly individual human life should be judged to be present two to three weeks after conception. My position recognizes that potentiality is present very early and much development occurs on the basis of what has been present from the very beginning. Later points of development are seen as constituting no more than developing stages and not crucial qualitative differences that are so significant as to determine the beginning of truly human life. Many who adopt this criterion choose the moment of fertilization or conception as the beginning of truly human life. From the first moment of conception there is a unique never-to-be-repeated genotype.

My position rests heavily on the concept of individuality. Individuality is not really present at the very beginning because twinning and recombination remain possible. Only after about three weeks is this individuality present. These arguments are buttressed by two other considerations—before this time the cells are pluripotential and cannot change without the appearance of the primary organizer which is not yet present. Also the many fertilized ova which, even in the normal process of reproduction, are spontaneously aborted before implanting in the uterus also tend to argue that we are not dealing here with truly individual human life. Although my position maintains that truly individual human life is not present until two to three weeks after conception, before this time the zygote, morula, and blastocyst do have some value and importance.[32]

II. Clinical In Vitro Fertilization and Embryo Transfer

All the questions considered thus far are related to the ethical decisions about *in vitro* fertilization and embryo transplant. Those who oppose obtaining the semen by masturbation or oppose AIH or believe that human life is present from the very moment of conception would logically be opposed to *in vitro* fertilization and embryo transfer under any circumstances. One should not be surprised to learn that Pope Pius XII in 1956 stated that experiments in artificial human fecundation *in vitro* must be rejected as immoral and absolutely illicit.[33] However, from the positions I have taken on the issues up to now, logically the question of *in vitro* fertilization and embryo transplant remains open. This section will now consider the ethical issues dealing specifically with our topic.

Discards and failures

In practice many fertilizations are usually done, but only one embryo is ultimately transferred. The remaining fertilized ova are then discarded. In the process of trying to implant the embryo there will also be many failures. What about the problem of these discards and failures? According to my position they do not constitute truly individual human life, but obviously these early embryos do have a value and importance. However, since they are not deserving of the protection of truly human life, some discards and failures cannot constitute an absolute condemnation of *in vitro* fertilization and embryo transplant. It could be judged that their loss is compensated for by the good to be attained if the *in vitro* fertilization and embryo transplant becomes successful. In this connection it is necessary to recall that even in the normal process of reproduction many fertilized ova do not implant and are lost. Despite a few contrary voices[34] the vast majority of authors recognize that a large proportion of fertilized ova are never implanted.[35] Means should be taken to insure that discards and losses are not excessive.

Risks to the child-to-be

What right do those generating new life have to expose the child-to-be to the risks of *in vitro* fertilization such as future abnormalities? Here again, it is necessary to recall that there are risks for the child-to-be in the normal process of reproduction.

For many ethicists and scientists, such as R. Edwards, there is no real problem here. The fetus after implantation can be monitored by all types of prenatal diagnosis such as ultrasonics and amniocentesis. If any abnormalities appear, the fetus can be aborted. Edwards concludes that the risks of abnormal offspring following embryo transfer would then be very small.[36]

However, from my perspective I cannot accept the general solution of abortion of deformed fetuses, since a truly individual human life is already present. My ethical analysis must then deal somewhat differently with the question of the risks to the child-to-be.

Can any reason justify exposing the child-to-be to some risk? The potential conflict exists between the desire of the parents (supposing now the case of a married couple) to have a child and the risks to the child-to-be. Do the parents have a right to have a child? In general, for all people one would have to deny that there is an absolute right to have a child. Catholic theology and discipline respond by saying that a married couple has a right to place that act (the marital act) which is apt for generation, but whether or not generation follows is beyond their control and their right. Nor can one say that parents have a right to do everything possible to have a child, for there are obvious limits.

However, the desire for a married couple to have a child is something intimately connected with the reality of their marriage. The Christian tradition recognizes that one of the goods of marriage involves offspring. There is a strong connection between children and marriage. The desire of a married couple to have a child is much different from the desire of a nonmarried person to have a child. In this context there can be justification in exposing the child-to-be to some risks. Even in normal reproduction there are such risks. I would conclude that the risks in *in vitro* fertilization and embryo transfer should be about the same as in the normal process. Unless this type of assurance can be given, the artificial procedures would be wrong because of the disproportionate danger of risk to the child-to-be. At the very minimum experimentation on lower animals must be done to such a degree as to give assurance that the risk to the child-to-be is proportionate—that is, about the same as in the normal process.

The nature of human parenthood

Does *in vitro* fertilization depersonalize marriage and parenthood? The origin of the child is separated from the sphere of the specifically marital (bodily, sexual) love. The child can undoubtedly be the result of a loving decision on the part of the parents, but the bodily aspect is missing. Aspects of this question have already been discussed in considering AIH and AID.

Some, echoing the fear of Pope Pius XII that the domestic hearth will be turned into a biological laboratory,[37] claim that the laboratory reproduction of human beings is no longer human reproduction.[38] Undoubtedly there are certain human values in the normal way of parenthood and reproduction. However, *in vitro* fertilization and embryo transfer are proposed only for that limited number of situations in which the normal process cannot take place. On the other hand, I object to the approach of Joseph Fletcher, who seems to prefer the control of technology to the genetic lottery of chance.[39]

Needs and priorities

In vitro fertilization and embryo transfer are now proposed as a remedy for infertile parents when the wife has occluded oviducts and therefore is unable to have a child. The problem of infertility due to occluded ducts might affect two percent of the female population. However, some of these people can be helped by reconstruction of the oviduct. *In vitro* fertilization and embryo transfer could be of great benefit to a very small percentage of parents who are unable to have a child of their own. In addition, this technique could be used for many other purposes. A woman who lacks oocytes of her own could have an embryo formed from her husband's sperm and a donor's ovum transferred into her body. A woman unable to support a pregnancy could use a surrogate mother.[40]

The question of priorities within medicine and science is intimately connected with the narrower question of the need for *in vitro* fertilization and embryo transfer. The danger constantly arises of giving so much attention to comparatively esoteric procedures that basic medical care (e.g., maternal and prenatal health care) tends to be neglected. Many today agree that more emphasis should be put on preventive health care and not as much on crisis intervention. However, the costs involved in *in vitro* fertilization and embryo transfer do not amount to that much compared to other, more esoteric medical technologies.

The wedge argument

One very important aspect which arises in both everyday conversation and in the more reflective literature can be summarized in what is often called the principle of the wedge or the slippery slope or the camel's-nose-in-the-tent argument. If we allow *a*, then we open the door to *x*, *y*, and *z*. As generally understood, this argument does not presuppose an absolute and logically necessary connection between the first step and the second (i.e., if you give someone an inch, they cannot logically claim a right to a mile). However, there is a tendency to move in this direction. Perhaps many of the arguments advanced for *a* could also be advanced for *x*, *y*, and *z* even though *a* logically differs from *x*, *y*, and *z*. The wedge argument must be analyzed and applied very carefully.[41] On the one hand the wedge can be readily employed to justify the *status quo*, while, on the other, history often shows there was more of a connection between the first step and the final outcome than had been anticipated. There are many different aspects of this problem involving possible abuses which deserve some discussion.

Now that the technology of *in vitro* fertilization and embryo transfer has been successfully accomplished, this technique could be used for many different purposes and reasons. These new technologies could be used as a way of improving the gene pool of the human race and making better people. Here it is important to recognize the distinction between positive and negative eugenics. For many reasons I am totally opposed to any type of positive eugenics. This new technology should be confined to helping people with infertility problems. In this way it could be possible to construct what might be called a firebreak, thereby preventing the gradually escalating uses of this technology to the point of great abuses.

At the present time requests are generally limited to do research on *in vitro* fertilization and preimplantation embryos. Once this research has been done and the technologies relatively perfected, there will be demands and requests to do research on the embryo after the time of implantation. Science is rightly striving for knowledge and truth, since such striving constitutes the very goal and lifeblood of scientific inquiry.

In theory one must firmly acknowledge that there are limits to the pursuit of truth. There are some things in sociology that we might never be able to learn because the only way to discover such truths might violate the right to privacy of certain individuals. Medical science itself recognizes some limits; for example, we could learn much more if we allowed medical experimentation on living human beings in the same way we experiment on animals.

From my ethical perspective truly individual human life is present two to three weeks after conception, or shortly after the implantation of the embryo. In my view experimentation after that time and attempts to culture embryos *in vitro* beyond this stage of development raise insurmountable ethical problems. I am fearful that such a step will come about, and I want to prevent it.

An important consideration must be the effect of the new reproductive technologies on the family. The family occupies a unique and very significant place and role in society. The bearing and rearing of children ordinarily take place within the family context. In the last few decades we have recognized many problems and changes involving the family in contemporary society. Single parent families have become more and more common and generally acceptable both in theory and in practice.

There is a legitimate concern that these new technologies might affect the family deleteriously. This can readily be avoided by limiting *in vitro* fertilization and embryo transfer to those who are truly involved in a family situation involving a heterosexual couple in an established relationship. In this way added pressures will not be put on family structures if these techniques are so limited.

Another problem concerns the very meaning of medicine and its purposes. Medicine, according to Paul Ramsey, exists to cure the medical ills of people but should not be used for nonmedical purposes or to fulfill people's wishes or desires.[42] Such reasoning involves serious flaws, but there is also an element of truth that cannot be ignored. In our everyday life even now we accept the fact that medicine deals with nonmedical problems and is not always used for strictly medical purposes. Cosmetic surgery constitutes one obvious example. This practical example finds theoretical grounding in an understanding of medicine as being at the service of the whole human person and not merely limited to the narrower range of the strictly medical aspects of the person.

Nevertheless, there would be obvious abuses if medical technology can be used to fulfull one's wishes and desires with no further qualification. It is necessary to look more deeply into the question of the wishes and desires for a child. As mentioned above, not even married couples possess an absolute right to have a child. However, a strong connection exists between marriage and children which distinguishes the desire of the married couple for a child from the desire of others. All admit that a married couple can use such means as fertility testing, fertility treatment, and arranging coitus at the proper time to help achieve their desire for a child. Most ethicians acknowledge that artificial insemination (for many, including myself at times, AID) is morally acceptable. The acceptance of *in vitro* fertilization and embryo transfer for married couples would not open the door to the danger that wishes and desires alone justify any medical treatment or intervention.

Another very significant danger involves our attitude toward the control of our offspring and our lives as well as our compassion and concern for the abnormal, the retarded, and all those who fall below the accepted standards of normality. In general we must be open to all legitimate attempts to overcome disease, abnormality, and suffering; but we must also recognize that in the end it will be impossible to exercise perfect control over our human existence. An unbalanced quest for the goal of perfect control would have deleterious effects on our compassion for those who are suffering which has traditionally been called a hallmark of Judaeo-Christian civilization. Newer discoveries such as reproductive technologies do not necessarily involve a lessened compassion and concern for the abnormal, but we must be ever vigilant in this matter.

There already exists a popularly accepted slogan that every child should be a wanted child. In many ways I agree with the sentiments behind such an adage, but I would have great difficulty in accepting the possibly broader indications that we can control everything about our offspring and our own lives. Experience reminds us there are many things that happen to us in life that we do not want. The reality and mystery of suffering will always accompany us in our living and in our dying. Human existence would be rather sterile if we were able to totally determine everything that happens to us.

Two other issues

The thrust of the argument proposed thus far, especially in view of the danger of excesses and abuses, has limited *in vitro* fertilization and embryo transfer to married couples. Now the question is explicitly raised about such reproductive technologies using donor sperm and/or donor oocytes. This procedure involves an extended form of AID with the possibility of a donor ovum as well as a donor sperm. From an ethical perspective I have already proposed that AID could sometimes be justified, although there are many ethically problematic issues involved. On the ethical level I am hesitant about the morality of embryo culture and transfer involving donor gametes. On the level of public policy at the present time I do not approve of *in vitro* fertilization and embryo transfer in these cases. There are many serious moral questions (not serious enough to constitute an absolute moral prohibition) involved in AID which are not present in AIH. As a matter of public policy it would be very difficult to monitor all these very significant problems. In addition there are still many legal questions about AID, so one should proceed rather cautiously in this area. In introducing new procedures involving the danger of abuses prudence seems to indicate a cautious approach.

Another question concerns a surrogate mother for those women who are unable or unwilling to carry their own children. Here again there is a slippery slope from being medically unable to being unwilling, whether for very serious or for frivolous reasons. There are serious reservations about such a procedure precisely because of the bodily relationship existing between the woman who carries the child and the child. Also there could be complicated and perplexing legal problems. By preventing such a procedure one also places a firm firebreak in the path of possibly spreading abuses of this new reproductive technology.

Ethical conclusions

In conclusion my analysis of the morality of *in vitro* fertilization and embryo transfer accepts such a procedure under the following conditions:

1. Discards and losses are minimized as much as possible.

2. There must be a proven assurance that the danger of harm to the child-to-be is about the same as in normal conception. A thorough investigation of all the available scientific data must be made to see if this condition exists at the present time.

3. The procedure is limited to an established heterosexual couple whose own sperm and ovum are fertilized *in vitro* and then transferred into the womb of the wife.

The discussion has generally been in terms of the clinical work done with individual patients. What about basic research in *in vitro* fertilization and transfer of preimplantation embryos? Almost all of the relevant issues have been discussed previously. In addition, the canon of informed consent with regard to experimentation is definitely called for in this case. Research can be done at the human level only after thorough research has been done on lower levels. The purpose of the research must be specifically stated, and the need for such research must be demonstrated. The nature of the matter involved in the research calls for respect and for economy to avoid unnecessary waste. The research should be restricted to preimplantation embryos, and any attempts to culture the fetus beyond this stage are wrong.

Legality and public funding

This chapter has addressed the question of *in vitro* fertilization and embryo transfer from an ethical perspective. What about public policy and public funding? There are three distinct issues involved here—morality, legality, and public funding. Is my moral position too liberal or too restrictive in terms of legality and public funding?

Some might argue that my position is too liberal in the light of the many people in our society who are opposed to such a technique. Some of them might be opposed because they believe truly human life is involved. Even in the light of my ethical position one could still conclude against the legality or especially against the public funding of such research and techniques. I would not make such judgments.

Is the ethical position taken here too restrictive for a public policy of acceptance and funding? There are many people who might object to the restrictions proposed in this paper—clinical work restricted to the ovum and sperm of husband and wife with the embryo transferred into the uterus of the wife; no surrogate mothers; no culturing of or experimentation with postimplantation fetuses.

Many reasons of a prudential nature support the position outlined above. In dealing with new technologies which have a great impact on life and society caution is in order. Many ethical theories give some, if not all, importance to consequences, but no one possesses the Solomonic wisdom to know what will be the consequences of these new technologies. It will be important to see what consequences occur from a somewhat restrictive approach before entertaining other possibilities.

An objection might be raised that I am unfairly thrusting my moral positions, especially on the question of the beginning of human life, on others and preventing them from acting in accord with a different understanding. There are a number of possible responses to such an objection. Some could reach the same conclusion on different grounds than the prudential reasons mentioned above. Others could conclude that there are many people who are deeply convinced that truly human life is present after implantation and public peace calls for respect for this position, especially when there are no overwhelming rights in collision with this understanding. Others could arrive at this same conclusion, not on the basis that truly human life is present in the postimplantation fetus, but on the basis that the fetus at that time in development has greater value than the reasons proposed for extending the culturing of embryos beyond this time.

There are significant differences between the law on abortion and policy on the legality and funding of research. Although I believe in a comparatively early time for the beginning of truly human life, I have accepted the Supreme Court's ruling on abortion law and opposed efforts to overturn this ruling through a constitutional amendment. In abortion the rights of the mother are involved. In our pluralistic society in which there is dispute about the beginning of human life I can understand a conclusion which says that the benefit of the doubt should be given to the rights of the mother and her freedom to act. However, in this case there is no conflict between the fetus and the rights of the mother or any strict human rights.

In conclusion this paper maintains that under certain conditions *in vitro* fertilization and embryo transfer are morally acceptable and also proposes this conclusion as a basis for public policy. However, a decision on funding requires a further discussion in the light of the principles of distributive justice and of the various human needs competing for funding.

NOTES

1. The characteristic Roman Catholic emphasis on human nature and human reason in ethics is universally recognized. From a Protestant perspective, see Roger Mehl, *Catholic Ethics and Protestant Ethics* (Philadelphia: Westminster Press, 1971) and especially James M. Gustafson, *Protestant and Roman Catholic Ethics: Prospects for Rapprochement* (Chicago: University of Chicago Press, 1978).

2. E.g., Gerald Kelly, *Medico-Moral Problems* (St. Louis: The Catholic Hospital Association, 1958). For a recent exception which bases its approach to *in vitro* fertilization on the

Christian content of the faith instinct, see Donald J. Keefe, "Biblical Symbolism and the Morality of *in vitro* Fertilization," *Theology Digest* 22 (1974), 308-323.

3. Josef Fuchs, *Esiste una morale cristiana?* (Rome: Herder, 1970). For a summary of this debate and a conclusion agreeing with mine, see Richard A. McCormick, "Notes on Moral Theology," *Theological Studies* 32 (1971), 71-78; 34 (1973), 58-61.

4. Pope Pius XII, "Allocution to the Fourth International Congress of Catholic Doctors," September 29, 1949; English translation: *The Human Body: Papal Teachings,* selected and arranged by the monks of Solesmes (Boston: St. Paul Editions, 1960), pp. 114-119. Artificial insemination was referred to in the following subsequent papal addresses of Pope Pius XII: "Allocution to Italian Midwives," October 29, 1951; English translation: *The Human Body,* pp. 149-178; "Allocution to the Second World Congress on Fertility and Sterility," May 19, 1956; English translation: *The Human Body,* pp. 384-394; "Allocution to the Seventh International Hematological Congress," September 12, 1958; English translation: *The Pope Speaks* 6 (1959-60), pp. 392-400. The official versions of these and other papal documents are found in *Acta apostolicae sedis.*

5. Paul Ramsey, *Fabricated Man: The Ethics of Genetic Control* (New Haven: Yale University Press, 1970).

6. Harvey Cox, *On Not Leaving It to the Snake* (New York: Macmillan, 1967). In later writings Cox has modified his understanding of anthropology and of eschatology.

7. Joseph Fletcher, "New Beginnings in Life: A Theologian's Response," in *The New Genetics and the Future of Man,* ed. Michael Hamilton (Grand Rapids, Michigan: William B. Eerdmans Publishing Co., 1971), pp. 78-89; Fletcher, *The Ethics of Genetic Control* (Garden City, New York: Doubleday Anchor Books, 1974).

8. For example, the vast majority of Catholic theologians believe that the papal condemnation of artificial contraception does not constitute an infallible teaching. A few view this teaching as infallible, not on the basis of inclusion in encyclicals, but because it has been constantly taught as such by the pope in union with the bishops throughout the world.

9. Franciscus X. Hürth, "Annotationes," *Periodica de re morali canonica liturgica* 41 (1952), 245-249.

10. Joseph A. Komonchak, "Ordinary Papal Magisterium and Religious Assent," in *Contraception: Authority and Dissent*, ed. Charles E. Curran (New York: Herder and Herder, 1969), pp. 101-126.

11. For a concise summary of the significant issues involved, see André E. Hellegers and Richard A. McCormick, "Unanswered Questions on Test Tube Life," *America* 139 (August 19, 1978), 74-78.

12. Thomas Aquinas, *Summa theologiae*, Ia-IIae, Prologue.

13. *Enchiridion symbolorum definitionum et declarationum de rebus fidei et morum*, ed. H. Denzinger, A. Schönmetzer, 32nd ed. (Herder: Barcelona, 1963), n. 3323. Hereafter cited as *D.S.*

14. The historical development of the teaching on artificial insemination has been traced in a number of different places. See William Kevin Grover, *Artificial Insemination among Human Beings* (Washington: The Catholic University of America Press, 1948); Hyacinthus M. Hering, *De fecundatione artificiali* (Rome: Officium Libri Catholici, 1952).

15. *D.S.*, n. 3684.

16. *The Human Body*, pp. 390-392.

17. Thomas J. O'Donnell, *Medicine and Christian Morality* (New York: Alba House, 1976), pp. 257-267. As O'Donnell points out, the older teaching was reaffirmed by the bishops of the United States in Directive 21 of *The Ethical and Religious Directives for Catholic Health Facilities* issued in November 1971.

18. E.g., Bernard Häring, *Medical Ethics* (Notre Dame, Indiana: Fides Publishers, 1973), pp. 92-93.

19. Arthur Vermeersch, *De castitate et vitiis oppositis* (Rome: Università Gregoriana, 1919), n. 241; Gerald Kelly, "The Morality of Artificial Insemination," *American Ecclesiastical Review* 101 (1939), 109-118.

20. For aspects of this debate, see *The Clergy Review* 23 (1943), 564; 25 (1945), 268-270, 335-336, 381-382; 29 (1948), 359-360; 30 (1948), 144, 357-358; also *Theological Studies* 8 (1947), 106-110; 10 (1949), 113-114.

21. *The Human Body*, p. 119. This translation is from Kelly, *Medico-Moral Problems*, pp. 229-230.

22. *The Human Body*, pp. 171-172. This translation is from the official N.C.W.C. translation.

23. John C. Ford and Gerald Kelly, *Contemporary Moral Theology* II: *Marriage Questions* (Westminster, Md.: Newman Press, 1963), pp. 289-290.

24. E.g., Rodger van Allen, "Artificial Insemination (AIH): A Contemporary Re-Analysis," *Homiletic and Pastoral Review* 70 (1969-1970), 363-372; Richard A. McCormick, "Notes on Moral Theology," *Theological Studies* 32 (1971), 94-97; Roger Troisfontaines, "L'insémination artificielle: problèmes éthiques," *Nouvelle revue théologique* 95 (1973), 764-778; Bernard Häring, *Ethics of Manipulation: Issues in Medicine, Behavior Control and Genetics* (New York: Seabury Press, 1975), pp. 194-198; John F. Dedek, *Contemporary Medical Ethics* (New York: Sheed and Ward, 1975), pp. 92-105.

25. *The Human Body*, p. 118.

26. For the description of such a clinic and an ethical position similar to my own, see René Simon, "Expérimentations et déplacements éthiques: a propos de l'insémination artificielle," *Recherches de sciences religieuse* 62 (1974), 515-539.

27. For example, McCormick, Häring, and Dedek have expressed such rejections of AID.

28. Karl Rahner, "The Problem of Genetic Manipulation," in *Theological Investigations* XI: *Writings of 1965-67, I* (New York: Herder and Herder, 1972), pp. 225-252.

29. James B. Nelson, *Human Medicine: Ethical Perspectives on New Medical Issues* (Minneapolis: Augsburg Publishing House, 1973), pp. 59-78; *Law and Ethics of AID and Embryo Transfer*, ed. G.E.W. Wolstenholme and D. Fitzsimons (Amsterdam: North-Holland Publishing Co., 1973).

30. Philippe Delhaye, "Le magistère catholique et l'avortement," *Ésprit et vie* 83 (1973), 434-436, 449-457.

31. I am summarizing here material presented in my article "Abortion: Contemporary Debate," *Encyclopedia of Bioethics* ed. Warren T. Reich (New York: Free Press-Macmillan, 1978), I, pp. 17-26.

32. For a similar position, see Gabriel Pastrana, "Personhood and the Beginning of Human Life," *The Thomist* 41 (1977), 247-294.

33. *The Human Body*, p. 389.

34. Thomas W. Hilgers, "Human Reproduction: Three Issues," *Theological Studies* 38 (1977), pp. 147-149.

35. E.g., C.J. Roberts and C.R. Lowe, "Where Have All the

Conceptions Gone?" *The Lancet* no. 7905 (March 1, 1975), 498-499.

36. R.G. Edwards, "Fertilization of Human Eggs *in vitro:* Morals, Ethics and the Law," *The Quarterly Review of Biology* 49 (1974), 9.

37. *The Human Body*, p. 171.

38. Ramsey, *Fabricated Man*, pp. 102-160; Ramsey, "Shall We 'Reproduce'? II: Rejoinders and Future Forecast," *Journal of the American Medical Association* 120 (June 12, 1972), 1481-1483; Leon Kass, "Making Babies—The New Biology and the 'Old' Morality," *The Public Interest* 26 (Winter, 1972), 48-50.

39. Fletcher, *Ethics of Genetic Control*, p. 36.

40. Edwards, "Fertilization of Human Eggs *in vitro*," p. 10.

41. For a discussion of the wedge argument, see Sissela Bok, "The Leading Edge of the Wedge," *The Hastings Center Report* 1, 3 (December 1971), 9-11; Paul Ramsey, "The Wedge: Not So Simple," *The Hastings Center Report* 1, 3 (December 1971), 11-12.

42. Ramsey, "Shall We 'Reproduce'?" p. 1481.

7. The Contraceptive Revolution and the Human Condition

The Council of the Society for Health and Human Values has determined that the most significant and far-reaching advance produced by the new biology is contraception. The purpose of this chapter is to study from the perspective of moral theology or Christian ethics the phenomenon of contraception—the great revolution of the new biology—and to see what this tells us about new images of the human condition.[1]

I. The Contraception Revolution

The fact of the contraception revolution must be admitted by all. In 1976 only 7.7 percent of American married women were classified as fertile, not wanting to become pregnant, and nonusers of contraception in their marriage.[2] The changes brought about by contraception have been enormous. At the family level in all parts of the world the procreation of offspring can now be controlled by the marriage partners. No longer are sexual relationships necessarily connected with procreation. Family planning has replaced biological necessity as the way in which parents bring children into the world. Such family planning has above all freed the woman from the biological necessity of spending most of her life as a bearer and nurturer of children. The ability to plan, to limit the number of children, or even to have no children at all has already contributed much to the changing role of women in contemporary society. However, in parts of the world there is still some resistance to family planning and the use of contraception.

Effective contraceptive methods have made it possible at least in theory for the population of countries and of the world to be controlled. According to the "World Population Plan of Action" adopted by the World Population Congress meeting in Bucharest in 1974 under the auspices of the United Nations, if the world population growth continues at the rate of 2 percent, which has been occurring since 1950, there would be a doubling of the world population every thirty-five years.[3] There are different theories about the meaning and extent of the population problem, but at the very minimum all recognize the need for population control in some countries of the world. Effective and cheap contraceptive devices make the control of population much easier.

For individuals engaging in sexual relations contraception does away with the fear of pregnancy. It is difficult to correlate the exact relationship between sexual activity among young nonmarrieds and contraception, but the general wisdom maintains that contraception has definitely contributed to the fact that more unmarried people are sexually active today than ever before. A recent study shows a remarkable upsurge in premarital intercourse by unmarried teen-aged women living in metropolitan areas. A survey taken in 1971 indicated that 30 percent of these young unmarried women had sexual intercourse by age nineteen. In 1976 the percentage rose to 43 percent. The latest survey puts the figure at 50 percent.[4]

The term "revolution" is often abused in our media conscious age, but perhaps the word is justified in referring to the use of contraception and the resultant change brought about for individuals, for families, and for nations in dealing with the problem of human control over births. Effective contraceptive devices have given human beings control over the procreative aspect of sexual relationships and have contributed greatly to significant societal changes. However, the contraceptive revolution has not been without its problems. There has been a number of significant debates in the area of contraception that can help us to evaluate better the whole question of contraception as an illustration of the ethical and human possibilities and dilemmas brought about by the new biology. The debates have centered on a number of issues—the morality of using contraception; the safety and side effects of contraceptive devices, especially the pill; the problems connected with population control; and the uses and abuses of the power of contraceptive technology.

The morality of contraception

The morality of using contraception as a means of family planning has been attacked primarily by the Roman Catholic Church. In 1968 Pope Paul VI reiterated the condemnation of artificial contraception in his encyclical *Humanae vitae*. The Catholic Church, however, believes in responsible parenthood. Couples should bring into the world only those children that they can care for and educate properly. As early as 1951 Pope Pius XII acknowledged that medical, eugenic, economic, and social conditions can justify the desire to limit the size of one's family. But the official hierarchical Catholic teaching does not allow the use of any means that interfere with the natural act of sexual intercourse or with the sexual faculty. The God-given purpose of the sexual faculty is for the procreation and education of offspring and for the love union of the spouses. Every act of sexual intercourse must be open to this twofold finality. Human beings cannot directly interfere with the faculty or with the act so that the natural finality is frustrated.[5]

There are both practical and theoretical objections to this official teaching within Roman Catholicism. Archbishop John Quinn of San Francisco, president of the National Conference of Catholic Bishops, has recognized the serious pastoral problems existing in the American church on this issue. Quinn recently quoted statistics showing that 76.5 percent of American Catholic married

women of child-bearing age use some form of contraception, and 94 percent of these were employing means
condemned by the pope. Many theologians have disagreed
with the conclusion and the reasoning proposed by the
pope. Human beings do have the power and responsibility to interfere with the sexual faculty and act. The official
Catholic teaching is often accused of a physicalism or
biologism because the biological or physical structure of
the act is made normative and cannot be interfered with.[6] I
take this dissenting position.

Some Catholics and others have been advocating natural family planning whereby a couple determines the time
of ovulation by an examination of the woman's cervical
mucus and limits conjugal relations to the sterile time.
Promoters of natural family planning (NFP) support this
approach with many reasons—often using arguments
proposed against other forms of contraception. Natural
family planning capitalizes on the contemporary appreciation of the natural, which seeks to avoid additives and
pills. NFP appeals to the hightest aspect of the human—
the love and discipline of the spouses—and is not merely a
scientific technique. The method is totally safe and avoids
many of the dangers often associated with the pill. NFP
requires the joint cooperation of both spouses and does
not put the burden of contraception on one—especially
the woman.[7] There do seem to be many attractive aspects
about NFP, but I personally see no moral problem in
using other forms of contraception as a means of exerci-
sing responsible parenthood. Unfortunately, NFP does
not appear to be effective where discipline, training, and
high motivation are not present, so that its effectiveness
with regard to population control is questionable.[8]

A related but different moral problem concerns the use
of contraception by unmarried people. Although a sur-
prising number of sexually active teenagers do not use
contraception, still there can be no doubt that the
availability of contraception has contributed to the growing frequency of extra and premarital sexual relations. In
general the Judaeo-Christian tradition has historically
condemned sexual relations outside the context of mar-

riage. The vast majority of philosophical and theological ethicists seem to agree in insisting that sexual relations must be seen in the context of person relations. Casual and impersonal sex violates the human meaning of sexuality. Many, myself included, understand the full meaning of human sexuality in terms of the total commitment of one person to another in marriage. On the other hand, while maintaining that casual and impersonal sex and sex without full personal commitment are morally wrong, I and many others would urge people engaging in such sexual intercourse to use contraception as a way of avoiding conception. Such people obviously are not prepared to bring children into the world and educate them.

Safety and side effects

The most discussed question in the area of oral contraception has been the safety and side effects of the pill. In a period of twenty years the pill has become the most widely used form of artificial contraception. Recent estimates (1978) from the World Health Organization indicate that somewhere between 50 and 80 million women in the world are using the pill. Not only is the pill effective, but it is now comparatively inexpensive. The cost of oral contraceptives in large government projects has been reduced to about fifteen cents per woman per month.[9] Effectiveness and availability are two very important characteristics significantly influencing the importance of the pill as a form of contraception. In the United States about half of all married women practicing contraception (as distinguished from sterilization) use the pill. However, there is a significant change in women aged 35 to 44. In this category over 50 percent of the married couples are sterile, and 28.9 of the total number of married couples are sterile because of contraceptive sterilization—either tubal ligation for the women or vasectomy for the males. Of the 49.9 percent of women in fertile marriages in this age bracket, 72 percent use contraceptives in their marriage. But only one out of five of these contraceptors uses the pill. These figures show the diminishing percentage of women over 35 years who use the pill apparently because of the health risk involved.[10]

The question of safety and risk has been a constant worry for women and also a matter for frequent discussion in both the scientific and popular literature. An article in the *New York Times Magazine* in 1976 accepted the conclusion proposed by Professor Martin Vessey of Oxford, whose study group based their findings on the medical histories of seventeen thousand users of the pill. The benefits of the pill outweigh its disadvantages, but there are some qualifications. Pill users should be kept under general supervision by their doctors. They should limit the length of time they stay on the pill. After 35 years, since the adverse effects tend to increase, for example, the risk of a thromboembolic event, other methods of contraception are suggested.[11]

A 1978 study by Mishell in the *American Journal of Diseased Children* listed the following absolute contra-indications for the pill: estrogen dependent neoplasia; cancer of the breast; active, acute, or marked chronic liver disease with abnormal function; a history of thrombophlebitis, thromboembolism, or thrombotic disease, including cerebral, vascular, and coronary artery disease; undiagnosed abnormal uterine bleeding; pregnancy; congenital hyperlipidemia; diabetes mellitus; history of gestational diabetes; hypertension. Relative contraindications include: depression, migraine headache, leiomyomata of the uterus, epilepsy, oligomenorrhea, amenorrhea. Note that in addition to the problems of safety and risk there also are the unwanted side effects such as possible weight gain, headaches, and menstrual irregularities. The study concludes that women over 35 years should discontinue oral contraceptives; women under 35 years with hypertension, diabetes, and hyperlipidemia and those who are heavy smokers should not use the steroid pills.[12]

The most intense study in the United States, conducted by the Kaiser-Permanente Medical Center at Walnut Creek, California, has involved more than sixteen thousand pill users over a period of ten years. The final report of this study, which will now cease because of its high cost (4.3 million dollars), is being readied for publication. Newspaper accounts report the findings that in a population of young, adult, white, middle-class women the risks of oral contraception use appear to be negligible. But the final word in not in, and women must weigh the pros and cons among the uncertainties. Smoking, long sun exposure, and having multiple sex partners increase the risks.[13]

However, there has been a continuing opposition to the use of the contraceptive pill, especially from some feminist groups who view the risks connected with the pill as unacceptable and unnecessary. There are other forms of safe contraception which do not put such a burden on the woman.[14]

One can conclude there will probably never be a form of contraception which is absolutely safe with no negative side effects and no inconveniences. The woman using the pill now must make a prudential judgment based on the available information. However, one should remember that there are also risks in childbearing itself.

The possible dangers and side effects connected with the pill have made the public and regulatory agencies, particularly the Food and Drug Administration (FDA), more conscious of the need for safety in the use of drugs in general and in the area of contraception especially. There is some dispute about whether the United States is too stringent in its requirements of testing before allowing new drugs and especially new forms of contraception to go on the market. Some even claim that under the present directives the original contraceptive pill would never have appeared. In the future it will be very difficult to come up with newer contraceptive pills and devices precisely because of the large cost involved in research and in the necessary testing before the pill could be approved.[15]

One very significant, continuing debate concerns the contraceptive Depo-Provera, which is injected intramuscularly in women and is effective for three months. Depo-Provera has not been approved by the FDA in the United States for contraceptive use, although is has been approved for use in treating advanced endometrial cancer. In the United States groups such as the National Women's Health Network have opposed the drug.[16] However, the medical board of the International Planned Parenthood Federation has endorsed the widespread use of Depo-Provera as a contraceptive.[17]

In general I support the strict testing standards and regulations which are now in effect. The danger is great that researchers and drug companies with their primary interest of marketing drugs as quickly as possible will tend not to recognize the need for adequate safeguards and testing before such drugs are put on the market. Government regulations with strict and fair procedures are absolutely necessary even though such testing will inevitably cause delays before drugs are used and will raise the cost of marketing new drugs.

There is one other "side effect" of the pill that should be mentioned, but with side effects understood in a broader way. This is the great rise in the rate of VD. In the mid-1950s there was a general feeling that VD was no longer a real problem in the United States. Federal appropriations for VD fell from a high of 17 million dollars to 3 million dollars in 1955. But in the late 1950s after the introduction of the pill the reported cases of infectious syphilis and gonorrhea began to rise. By the 1970s gonorrhea had become the number one of all the reportable communicable diseases in the United States. Similar growth in VD has been reported in other countries of the first world such as England, Canada, Australia, and Denmark.[18] One can legitimately presume that the use of the pill is causally related in some manner to the increase in VD because the pill (unlike the condom) does nothing to prevent the spread of VD. The linkage between the use of the pill and the rise of VD is another indication that there is no such thing as a contraceptive which is perfect from every perspective.

Population control

The macro aspects of the contraception revolution involve especially the question of population control.

Here, too, there has been much discussion in the last decades. Of primary importance is the very definition and understanding of the problem itself. I agree with the approach of Philip Hauser, who insists on a complex understanding of the problem, including four elements or even four crises. The population explosion refers to the growing number of people. The population implosion indicates the increasing concentration of people on relatively small portions of the earth's surface. The population displosion means the increasing heterogeneity of people who share the same geographical state as well as the same social, political, and economic conditions, as exemplified by current problems in Northern Ireland, in many African countries, and even in Canada. Finally, the technoplosion refers to the accelerated pace of technological innovation which has characterized our present era. Hauser maintains that the problems created or exacerbated by implosion and displosion will create more human misery during the remainder of this century than the problems produced by excessive fertility and growth.[19] However, we must not forget the long-range problems.

A fundamental ethical problem concerns the means used by governments to control the growth of population. The moral values involved here are the freedom of the individual, justice, and the general welfare of the nation, including security and survival.[20] On a scale of government interference in a continuum from freedom to coercive policies, the following general approaches can be identified: education, motivation, and propaganda for population control together with provision of acceptable means to control fertility to all who want them; change of structures which affect demography; incentives offered to control population; coercive methods.[21]

In general I am opposed to coercive measures except as an absolutely last resort, but it is necessary to evaluate properly the role and meaning of freedom in these discussions about contraception and population control. Too often freedom in these matters can be poorly understood in an overly individualistic sense. Insistence on reproductive autonomy can forget the social dimensions of human sexuality and procreation. Sexuality and procreation involve a relationship to the human species. Precisely because of the social aspects of procreation the individual couple must give consideration to the broader question of overpopulation. The possibility of accepting coercion as a last resort, at least from a theoretical position, is based on this more social understanding of freedom and responsibility in the matter of marriage. However, in practice, the complexity of the population problem and the dangers of abuse argue against the acceptance of coercion.

The reasoning behind the official Catholic Church's teaching on procreation and its condemnation of artificial contraception is most instructive in this matter of freedom. The Catholic condemnation of artificial contraception rests on the assumption that the sexual faculty has a purpose and finality related to the species and including more than merely the individual or the couple. Freedom of the spouses is not the only ethical concern; the species must also be considered. The official Catholic approach is insightful in recognizing the need to consider more than the freedom of the spouses. Apart from the question of the means employed, the official Catholic position can and does support the need to control population if this is truly necessary for the human good. Catholic teaching in this and other related matters has never absolutized the freedom of the individual person but has constantly stressed the social nature of human existence. As mentioned above, I disagree with the aspect of official Catholic teaching which maintains that every single act must be open to procreation so that one cannot directly interfere with artificial means.

Contraception as power

In the last few decades there has been a growing skepticism and criticism of science and technology. Much of the recent ferment surfaced again at the Conference on Faith, Science, and the Future sponsored by the World Council of Churches at the Massachusetts Institute of Technology in July 1979. One of the most significant divergencies in the conference, in the preparatory papers, and in meetings concerns the very meaning of science itself. Note that we are not talking about technology as applied science but rather about pure science itself. The one perspective, which has been typical of traditional Western understanding, sees science as an objective search for knowledge and a method for solving problems. The objectivity of science calls for the scientist to abandon all subjective prejudices and presuppositions and enter into give-and-take with fellow scientists in the objective and disinterested search for truth. The method of test and experiment facilitates this objective search. Yet there is no doubt that science itself can and has been abused. The tremendous cost of scientific research today means that pure science is subject to the industries and governments which support it. Likewise, the results of science and the technology it produces have been abused and put to wrong purposes. In this connection one can mention the question of atomic and nuclear weapons.[22]

A second view, often connected with a more radical perspective, sees science not so much as knowledge but as power. The sociology of knowledge reminds us that knowledge is always a function of practical interests. Science is power over nature and over people wielded by the strong against the weak. Science is what scientists do in the social situations in which they work. Science objectively exists only as a social reality and is closely related to economic and political interests. The objectivity and disinterestedness of science are a myth.[23]

Both positions seem to have some truth, but it is not necessary for us to become involved in a long discussion of the problem, since we are dealing with contraceptive technology, or applied science. All must recognize the connection between power and contraceptive technology. An examination of some of the debates in the matter of contraception shows that contraceptive technologies have constituted a power which has been used against the weak and the disadvantaged. Aspects of contraception as power have arisen vis-à-vis individual poor in this country, against women in general, and against the developing nations of the world.

First of all, contraception as power has been used against the poor in this country. Perhaps the best illustration has been the sterilization of people against their will. Headlines were created with the revelation that people in Virginia public institutions had been sterilized without their consent. Questions have also been raised about the free consent given by poor women to sterilizations when they did not truly understand the nature of the operation.[24] The dangers here are very real, and there have been many illustrations of such abuses of power without the truly informed consent of the persons involved.

Second, some feminists have maintained that women have been victimized by the pill. Men have used their dominant power to make sure that it is the woman who puts up with the risks of using the pill. While many look upon the pill as something which has brought about greater freedom for women, these feminists see the pill as another form of male oppression forcing the woman to take all the risks involved in contraception. Feminists and others also resent the importance given to the psychological fears often mentioned as deterring the male from sterilization, even though male sterilization (vasectomy) is a much simpler medical procedure than female sterilization (tubal ligation). Contraception can become another form of male dominance.[25]

A third aspect of contraception as power is seen in the attitudes of many of the countries of the first world to the population problems in the developing nations. Too often official United States policy and the opinions of many Americans, especially before the 1974 United Nations Conference in Bucharest adopted its World Population Plan of Action, saw the solution of the overpopulation problem only in terms of a reduction of the birth rate through efficient, inexpensive, and readily available contraception. Population growth was seen as the cause of many other problems such as retarded economic growth, shortage of food resources, pollution of the environment. One can readily recognize the temptation of employing a technological fix without realizing the complexity of the reality involved and above all without acknowledging the many problems created by the United States and other nations of the first world.

The complexity of the population problem is such that merely providing the means for individuals to control fertility is not enough. Other population factors are involved such as population distribution and structure, migration, mortality rates, and the role of women in society. Above all, the position of Americans with their unilateral approach to the population problem was suspect precisely because they failed to recognize the underlying problems to which the first world is contributing so much. Overconsumption by the first world creates just as many, if not more, problems than overpopulation by others. Above all the population question cannot be viewed apart from its interdependence with social phenomena such as economic change, environmental factors, and technological developments.[26]

There is some evidence to support the position that programs aimed at lowering fertility will not be successful unless they are accompanied by social and economic changes. To poverty-striken mothers in American ghettos a child is a source of joy, hope, and contentment which cannot be had in any other ways.[27] India's programs for population control based on massive contraception and sterilization have been failures apparently because they did not recognize the interrelatedness of the population problem with other factors, especially the economic.[28] One can understand how the poorer nations of the world saw in the American insistence on contraception and sterilization as the solution to the population problem another instance of the strong trying to hold on to their power and oppress the weak.

II. The Human Condition

What does this analysis of the contraceptive revolution and the ethical questions raised by it tell us about our image of the human condition? Our understanding of the human condition obviously influences our evaluation of contraceptive technology, but an analysis of the contraceptive revolution and its human and ethical ramifications also sheds some light on our appreciation of the human condition. Three different aspects of the human condition will be discussed—anthropology in general, human progress, and technological progress.

Anthropology

As might be expected, there have been and are different approaches to anthropology in the Christian tradition, and these differences continue to exist today. In general, one can distinguish more optimistic anthropologies and more pessimistic anthropologies. Harvey Cox with his emphasis on the secular city represented a more optimistic anthropology in his writings in the 1960s.[29] Cox did not deny the reality of sin, which in Christian theology has usually been the grounding for more pessimistic anthropology, but Cox attempted to reinterpret the very meaning of sin. The Christian tradition sees the primary sin of human beings as pride—the unwillingness to accept the limitations and dependency of our human condition. The good Christian thus becomes the individual who does not expect too much of oneself and is content to live within limitations. But today we need a doctrine of sin that will not encourage defense and dependency. We need an anthropology that will accentuate the responsibility that human beings must take for the cosmos and its future. An emphasis on guilt and forgiveness has made Christians look backward, but the gospel is a call to leave what is behind and open ourselves to the promises of the future. The primary sin is not pride but sloth—*acedia*—an abdication of our power and a failure to take responsibility for the world in which we live. Today the gospel calls the Christian to an adult stewardship, originality, inventiveness, and the control of the world. Even the sin of Adam and Eve was not pride but sloth. Self-doubt, hesitant activity, and dependency preceded that fatal nibble.[30]

Paul Ramsey, especially in his writings on the new biology, takes a more pessimistic view of anthropology and stresses that *hubris,* or pride, is the primary sin of human beings. Ramsey sees many ethical violations on the horizontal plane of human existence brought about by the new biology—coercive breeding or nonbreeding, injustices done to individuals or mishaps, the violation of the nature of human parenthood. All these ethical violations on the horizontal plane point to a fundamental flaw in the vertical dimension—*hubris,* or playing God. In attempts of the new biology to fabricate human beings, to prevent aging, to make cyborgs, to control intimate human moods and powers, Ramsey perceives the human desire to have limitless dominion over our lives—the fatal flaw of *hubris,* or the denial of our own creatureliness. Ramsey insists on the limitations of human wisdom as a guide for the rosy future portrayed by the messianic positivists. If our genetic planning policy is no better than our foreign policy or our urban policy, then we will truly be in trouble. Human beings must be willing to accept our finitude and our limitations, to say nothing of our sinfulness.[31]

My understanding of Christian anthropology is greatly influenced by what is logically the first step in any theological ethics—what has been called the stance, perspective, posture, or horizon of Christian ethics. The stance is the logically first step broad enough to encompass the entire matter of Christian ethics but also able to provide a perspective within which the field of moral theology can be viewed. As a stance for Christian ethics I proposed in chapter three the need to see all human reality in terms of the fivefold Christian mysteries of creation, sin, incarnation, redemption, and resurrection destiny. In the light of this stance anthropology tends to find a balance between the extremes of Cox and Ramsey as mentioned above. Creation, incarnation, and redemption all point to human goodness and the power which is ours as God's gracious gift. However, creation also reminds us of our finitude and limitations; sin affects us without ever destroying our basic goodness and without totally escaping the reality of redemption; resurrection destiny as the fullness of the kingdom always lies beyond our attainment in this world.

Such a theoretical framework for anthropology, which recognizes the positive aspects of human existence but also cautions about continuing limitation, sinfulness, and incompleteness, is confirmed by our consideration of contraceptive technology and by developments in the new biology. Human beings through technology have a greater power and corresponding responsibility than we ever had before. With the new medical technology human beings are called upon to make decisions about life and death itself, e.g., pulling the plug on the respirator or deciding who will receive lifesaving technologies. But, on the other hand, finitude and sinfulness will always affect our human existence. Contraception has enhanced human responsibility and freed us from a determinism by the forces of nature, but biological or any other kind of technology cannot overcome our basic creatureliness. Likewise, the proclivity to abuse based on our continuing sinfulness must always be recognized. Contraception, despite its many contributions to human development, has also contributed somewhat to a depersonalization of human sexuality in some areas of human behavior. Technological contraceptive power has been used by the strong at the expense of the weak. A series of checks and balances on researchers, drug companies, and contraception programs of governments is an absolute necessity.

The recognition of the greater power and responsibility that human beings have achieved because of science, technology, and other developments has led some to describe the human being as a self-creator. In one sense the concept of the human person as a self-creator is not all that new. Thomas Aquinas grounded his anthropology in a similar concept. In the prologue to the second part of the *Summa theologiae* which describes the ethical life, Aquinas briefly explains that he will now consider the human being who is an image of God precisely because the human being is endowed with intellect, free will, and the power of self-determination.[32] In contemporary theology Karl Rahner has emphasized the concept of the person as a self-creator. Such assertions must be properly understood. Rahner does not mean to deny all creaturely limitation, but he emphasizes that the human person truly creates and determines one's own self and subjectivity by one's free action. The German theologian stresses that the new aspect in this concept today is the fact that our transcendental self-manipulation can take on new historical and categorical forms because of our science and technology, especially in the biological area.[33] Rahner's emphasis on the subject is part of his transcendental approach, which can be criticized for not giving enough importance to the physical, social, political, and cosmic dimensions of human existence. However, Rahner would agree that we cannot speak of the human person as a self-creator understood in terms of one who makes something out of nothing. Human beings today, thanks to science and technology, have great power over our world, our environment, and even our bodies, but we can never deny our creaturely existence and limitations.

Intimately connected with the improper notion of the person as a self-creator is the ethical reductionism of seeing the human being only in terms of freedom. A proper human anthropology must recognize both our freedom and our limits. We are embodied spirits living in multiple relationships with others. As already pointed out in our discussion of contraceptive technology, a stress on individual freedom and autonomy has often failed to recognize that procreation involves us in a broader web of human relationships. Procreation can never be adequately considered only under the rubric of the freedom of the individual person or couple.

We do not exist in the world apart from our bodies, and to a certain extent we are limited by the givenness of our bodies. The official Catholic teaching condemns contraception as an unwarranted interference in the bodily structures of human existence. I do not agree with such a position, but I also do not agree with those who fail to recognize both the importance and the limitations of the bodily. Joseph Fletcher, for example, maintains that laboratory reproduction is more human than sexual reproduction precisely because it is more rational.[34] However, the bodily is a part of the human, and there are limitations connected with our body that we cannot forget. Fatigue and pain are two readily experienced limitations with which we constantly live. In the discussion of contraceptive technologies the best illustration of bodily limitations is the problem with the safety and side effects of the pill. The complex hormonal systems of the human body cannot be interferred with at will. There are intricate relationships and connections that must be taken into account. The chemicals that prevent ovulation can and do have deleterious effects on other bodily organs and functions. These limitations of the complex bodily system are analogous to the limitations of the "eco-systems" in our cosmos. The ecological crisis has made us aware of these continuing material limitations of the cosmic world that we inhabit. By overstressing our dominion, our power, and our freedom to intervene in our natural world, we fail to give due importance to the limitations inherent in our bodies and in our cosmos. Yes, human beings have great power and responsibility, but we also have limits, and true responsibility calls for us to recognize these limits.

Human progress

The question of human progress is ultimately connected with anthropology. What about human progress, especially in the light of the contraceptive revolution? Christian theology has taken a number of different approaches to human progress. In the early part of the twentieth century liberal Protestantism in general and the social gospel in particular emphasized human progress. Influenced by the theory of evolution and recent technological developments, these theologians accepted an evolutionary human progress, some even going so far as to accept the inevitability of such progress.[35]

Protestant liberalism was severely challenged by Karl Barth in Germany and by Reinhold Niebuhr in the United States. It was no coincidence that Barth's commentary on the Epistle to the Romans appeared in 1919,[36] and Niebuhr's *Moral Man and Immoral Society* was published in 1932.[37] The horror of the First World War burst the bubble of an optimistic progress which, according to the caricature, proclaimed that everyday and in every way we were becoming better and better. The brutal reality of war contradicted the bland slogans of the social gospel—the fatherhood of God and the brotherhood of men. It is a sad commentary that the sharpest attack in the United States against the progressivism of liberal Protestantism was occasioned by the economic problems of the depression rather than by the war! But, whatever the occasion, the progressive and optimistic theology of the early part of the century was no longer acceptable in the light of the brutality of war and the harshness of the industrial revolution with its ever-widening gulf between the rich and the poor. The neoorthodoxy of Barth and the Christian realism of Niebuhr stressed the transcendence of God rather than immanence, placed heavy emphasis on human sinfulness, and insisted that the fullness of the kingdom lies beyond the world, or "beyond tragedy" as Niebuhr entitled one of his books of sermons.[38] The Second World War reinforced the mood of realism with its denial of dramatic human progress within history.

In the 1960s a change occurred which can be seen in the theology of secularity and the death of God theology.[39] Secularity was no longer something opposed to the gospel, but the gospel according to the theologians of secularity calls for us to accept secularity with all its hopes and promises. The older pessimistic theology no longer attracted universal support, especially in the light of the power and the responsibilities that were in the hands of human beings to shape their own future and the destiny of the world. There are those who said that the secular city theology was just a warmed-over version of the social gospel, but it captured the attention of many in the middle 1960s.[40]

Once again, however, human experience shifted. The
great hopes of the early 1960s, as expressed for example in
the inaugural addresses of John F. Kennedy in 1960 and
Lyndon Johnson in 1964, were dashed against the stark
realities of discrimination, war, and poverty. Many thought
that the school desegregation decision of 1954 and the
march on Selma marked the beginning of a new era in race
relations, but the urban riots of the late 1960s reminded
Americans of how deeply racism and poverty were en-
grained in our society. The 1960s began with great hopes
of peace throughout the world, but the involvement in
Vietnam disillusioned many Americans. On a worldwide
basis the poverty problem indicated the structural problems of economic neocolonialism, because of which the
first world was systematically keeping the developing
world in the shackles of poverty. In the light of many of
these developments the overly optimistic theology of the
early 1960s was no longer convincing.

Changing attitudes to human progress from the 1960s
to the present can be seen in the work of many theologians. Take, for example, Johannes Metz. In the early
1960s Metz put heavy emphasis on secularity and the
world as history. This incarnational approach with its
stress on history rather than on nature emphasized human
freedom and responsibility in the world in which we
live.[41] By the middle 1960s Metz's understanding of the
problematic shifted from secularity to futurity, from an
incarnational to an eschatological approach. Eschatology,
futurity, and hope characterized the work of many theologians in this period. In this eschatology there was some
continuity between the present and the future.[42] In the
early 1970s a change emerged in Metz's development. The
tone becomes more pessimistic as the aspect of suffering is
added. The relationship of human beings to history now
occurs through suffering, which is seen in the light of the
dangerous memory of Jesus.[43] Finally in the later 1970s
the eschatological element in Metz now emphasizes not
the continuity but the discontinuity between the present
and the future. Apocalyptic becomes a central theme in
Metz, who strongly opposes an evolutionary and teleo-

logical view of eschatology which is often associated with the Western technological perspective.[44]

Thus we are confronted with the question: Is there truly human progress in history and how does it occur? Again, my theoretical approach is based on the stance or perspective. The goodness of creation, the incarnation, and the fact that redemption has already occurred argue for some continuity between the present and the future of the kingdom. However, human finitude, sinfulness, and resurrection destiny as future call for some discontinuity between the present and the future. The fullness of the kingdom is always beyond our grasp. Such a perspective has room for some truly human progress in history, but the negative aspects of finitude, sin, and eschatological incompleteness are limits against a naive, evolutionary, and too optimistic view of human progress. Such a perspective, especially when looking at history in the long view, does not expect to see any great or dramatic breakthroughs in human progress. Yes, there can and will be some limited progress over time, but there will be no utopias existing in this world. My approach thus differs from both evolutionary progressivism and contemporary apocalypticism.

How does this theoretical view of human progress stand up in the light of experience in history? The interpretation of history is always risky. One can point to great deformations that have occurred in the development of history. Modern war with its nuclear weapons has become infinitely more destructive than earlier wars. However, I think there has been limited but significant historical advance in terms of truly human progress. A very basic ethical reality concerns the rights, dignity, and equality of human beings. Here one can note some true historical progress. Slavery is nowhere near as prevalent as it was at one time. Our society today is much more aware of the equal rights of women. Contemporary human beings have a greater area in which to exercise their freedom and responsibility in many aspects of human life. Democratic government has given individuals a greater participation in their government. The Declaration of Human Rights

of the United Nations points to an ever-growing awareness on the international level of basic human rights.
Without claiming any utopian or dramatic breakthroughs
one can make an argument for some true but limited
human progress in history.

It seems as if theology has somewhat flip-flopped in its
approach to human progress and has been too easily
influenced by the immediate situations of the times. There
will always be more optimistic and more pessimistic
periods in human history, but a theological worldview
must be supple enough to recognize these ups and downs
without losing sight of the overall perspective which in
my judgment recognizes some true but limited progress in
the course of history. Struggle, with penultimate victories
somewhat outweighing penultimate defeats, will characterize our historical existence.

Technological progress

What is the relationship between technological progress and truly human progress? One significant factor
contributing to the optimistic understanding of human
progress in the 1960s was technological progress. There
can be no doubt that technology has made great progress.
Human beings have come from the discovery of the wheel
to the animal drawn cart, to the steam engine, the
automobile, the airplane, and the rocket ships that landed
human beings on the moon. Technological developments
seem to be ever progressive in the sense that new developments build on older discoveries and constantly move
forward as illustrated in the case of transportation.
However, the experience of the late 1960s and the 1970s
caused many to take a quite critical look at technological
progress.

First, technological progress is not the same as human
progress. The apparently steadily progressive thrust of
technological progress is not true of human progress.
Newer technology always builds on the old and improves
on it, but look at other areas of human existence. Why do
we still read Shakespeare, listen to Bach and Beethoven,
admire the sculpture of ancient Greece and Rome, and

recognize the artistry of Michelangelo or Raphael? Literature, art, drama, and music do not show this always-advancing progress which is true of science and technology. Human progress and technological progress are not the same precisely because the technological is only one small part of the human. Technology is never going to solve the great human problems of life and death, love and sharing, hope and endurance. Yet technology is not something evil or necessarily opposed to the human, but rather science and technology are the result of human creativity and therefore good. However, science and technology are also quite limited in terms of the truly and fully human. Since the human encompasses much more than the technological, the human at times must say no to the possibilities of technology.

Second, technological progress is not as unilaterally progressive and developmental as was supposed. Technological progress itself is ambiguous. Developments in transportation were used to illustrate the presumably always progressive nature of technological development, but later experience and reflection recall some negative aspects of such development. Think, for example, of the problem of air pollution or the flight from the cities occasioned by the mass use of automobiles. Technological advances, even apart from their relationship to the wider aspect of the human, are not without ambiguous side effects.

III. Conclusion

This paper has studied the contraceptive revolution and has analyzed the understanding of anthropology and of human and technological progress from the perspective of theological ethics. In light of all these considerations, some conclusions can now be drawn with regard to contraceptive technology and its relationship to the human.

First, contraceptive technology in general has been good for human beings. The effects of contraception in the matter of family planning and population control have been very beneficial. To free human beings from physical necessity and to give them greater control and responsibility enhances the reality of the human. The very term "responsible parenthood," accepted by about all people today, calls attention to the human good which has been brought into being by contraceptive technology.

Second, contraceptive technology is a limited human good. Technology itself can never solve or even touch the deeper human questions and problems of life and death, loving concern, or egoism. Contraception can contribute to the well being of spouses and of families. Population control can help nations and the whole world. However, the human problems and possibilities facing individuals, spouses, nations, and the world transcend the level of biological technologies or of all technologies combined. Recall the dangerously unilateral approach which viewed the problems of limiting population in the narrow terms of providing safe, cheap, and effective contraceptives and failed to recognize the many other aspects of the problem.

Third, this limited human good remains somewhat ambiguous. The best example of the ambiguity in contraceptive advances had been the dangers and side effects associated with the pill. There will undoubtedly never be a perfect contraceptive in the sense of something that is perfect from every single perspective—the hygenic, the eugenic, the aesthetic, etc. At the very minimum all existing contraceptive technologies seem to have some limitations and imperfections about them.

Fourth, contraception is a limited good which can be abused. While contraception has made it possible for people to practice responsible parenthood, it has also made it somewhat easier for others to engage in impersonal and irresponsible sexuality. Limited human goods are always subject to such abuse.

Fifth, contraceptive technology is susceptible to takeover by the strong at the expense of the weak. The poor in our country, women in general, and the poor nations of the world have all been victims of the contraceptive technology of the powerful. Thus contraceptive technology has been a good for human beings but a good that is somewhat limited, ambiguous, and vulnerable to take-over by the powerful at the expense of the weak. This assessment and understanding of contraceptive technology should provide us with a framework for judging the newer biological technologies that will come our way in the future.

NOTES

1. This chapter was originally presented at the annual meeting of the Society for Health and Human Values in October 1980. Throughout this article contraception will be used in the strict sense to include both contraception and sterilization but *not* abortion.

2. Kathleen Ford, "Contraceptive Use in the United States, 1973-1976," *Family Planning Perspectives* 10 (1978), 264-269.

3. United Nations Economic and Social Council, "World Population Plan of Action," *World Population Conference* (October 2, 1974), E/5585, par. n. 3.

4. Melvin Zelnik and John F. Kantner, "Sexual Activity, Contraceptive Use and Pregnancy among Metropolitan Area Teenagers: 1971-1979," *Family Planning Perspectives* 12 (1980), 230-237.

5. For a summary of this hierarchical Catholic teaching, see Thomas J. O'Donnell, *Medicine and Christian Morality* (Staten Island, New York: Alba House, 1976), pp. 238-257.

6. Archbishop John R. Quinn, "New Context for Contraception Teaching," *Origins: N.C. Documentary Service* 10 (October 9, 1980), 263-267. For an overview of the discussion within Catholicism on the occasion of the encyclical *Humanae vitae,* see William H. Shannon, *The Lively Debate: Response to Humanae Vitae* (New York: Sheed and Ward, 1970); Joseph A. Selling, "The Reaction to *Humanae Vitae:* A Study in Special and Fundamental Theology" (S.T.D. diss., Catholic University of Louvain, 1977).

7. Mary Shivanandan, *Natural Sex* (New York: Rawson, Wade Publishers, 1979).

8. World Health Organization, *Special Programme of Research, Development and Research Training in Human Reproduction*, 7th Annual Report, Geneva, November 1978. This report is quoted in Carl Djerassi, *The Politics of Contraception* (New York: W.W. Norton, 1980), pp. 9-10. For a defense of the effectiveness of NFP, see Shivanandan, *Natural Sex*.

9. Djerassi, *The Politics of Contraception*, p. 33.

10. Ford, *Family Planning Perspectives* 10 (1978), 264-369; Djerassi, *The Politics of Contraception*, pp. 33ff.

11. Paul Vaughan, "The Pill Turns Twenty," *The New York Times Magazine*, June 13, 1976, pp. 9ff. The scientific source for *The New York Times Magazine* article is M.P. Vessey and R. Doll, "Is the Pill Safe Enough to Continue Using?" *Proceedings of the Royal Society of London*, vol. B.195 (1976), 69-80.

12. David R. Mishell, "Contraception," *American Journal of Diseases of Children* 132 (September 1978), 912-921.

13. *The Washington Post*, Tuesday, October 21, 1980, p. A7.

14. Barbara Seaman, *The Doctor's Case against the Pill* (New York: Doubleday, 1980).

15. Djerassi, *The Politics of Contraception*, pp. 67-167.

16. Carol Levine, "Depro-Provera and Contraceptive Risk: A Case Study of Values in Conflict," *The Hastings Center Report* 9, 4 (August 1979), 8-11.

17. *The New York Times*, October 19, 1980, section 1, p. 56.

18. Louis Lasagna, *The VD Epidemic* (Philadelphia: Temple University Press, 1975), pp. 1-11.

19. Philip M. Hauser, "Population Criteria in Foreign Aid Programs," in *The Population Crisis and Moral Responsibility*, ed. J. Philip Wogaman (Washington: Public Affairs Press, 1973), pp. 233-239.

20. This is the conclusion of the Population Research Group of the Institute of Society, Ethics and the Life Sciences, which was charged by the Commission on Population Growth and the American Future to examine the relevant ethical values and principles. See *Population Policy and Ethics: The American Experience*, ed. Robert M. Veatch (New York: Irvington Publishers, 1977), especially pp. 477-484.

21. Robert M. Veatch, "An Ethical Analysis of Population Policy Proposals," in *Population Policy and Ethics*, pp. 445-475.

22. Robert Hanbury Brown, "The Nature of Science," in *Faith and Science in an Unjust World: Report of the World Council of Churches' Conference on Faith, Science and the Future*, vol. I, *Plenary Sessions*, ed. Roger L. Shinn (Philadelphia: Fortress Press, 1980), pp. 31-40.

23. Ruben Alves, "On the Eating Habits of Science," in *Faith and Science in an Unjust World*, pp. 41-43.

24. *The Washington Post*, February 23, 1980, p. Al. Patricia Donovan, "Sterlizing the Poor and Incompetent," *The Hastings Center Report* 6, 5 (October 1976), 7, 8; see also the symposium "Sterilization of the Retarded: In Whose Interest?" *The Hastings Center Report* 8, 3 (June 1978), 28-41.

25. See Seaman, *The Doctor's Case against the Pill.*

26. United Nations Economic and Social Council, "World Population Plan of Action," *World Population Conference* (October 2, 1974), E/5585, par. nn. 20-67. For other authors who stressed the multidimensional aspects of the problem, see Donald P. Warwick, "Ethics and Population Control in Developing Countries," *The Hastings Center Report* 4, 3 (June 1974), 1-4; Peter J. Henriot, "Global Population in Perspective: Implications for U.S. Policy Response," *Theological Studies* 35 (1974), 48-70.

27. Arthur J. Dyck, "American Global Population Policy: An Ethical Analysis," *Linacre Quarterly* 42 (1975), 60.

28. John F.X. Harriott, "Bucharest and Beyond," *The Month* 7 (1974), 630.

29. Harvey Cox, *The Secular City: Secularization and Urbanization in Theological Perspective* (New York: Macmillan, 1965).

30. Harvey Cox, *On Not Leaving It to the Snake* (New York: Macmillan, 1967), pp. ix-xix.

31. Paul Ramsey, *Fabricated Man: The Ethics of Genetic Control* (New Haven: Yale University Press, 1970), especially pp. 90-96, 150-160.

32. *Summa theologiae*, I*a*-II*ae*, Prologue.

33. Karl Rahner, *Theological Investigations*, vol. IX, *Writings of 1965-1967, I* (New York: Herder and Herder, 1972), pp. 205-252.

34. Joseph Fletcher, "Ethical Aspects of Genetic Controls: Designed Genetic Changes in Man," *New England Journal of*

Medicine 285 (September 30, 1971), 780, 781; see also Fletcher, *The Ethics of Genetic Control: Ending Reproductive Roulette* (Garden City, New York: Doubleday Anchor Books, 1974).

35. For an overview of this period in Protestantism, see John Dillenberger and Claude Welch, *Protestant Christianity: Interpreted through Its Development* (New York: Charles Scribner's Sons, 1954), pp. 160-254.

36. Karl Barth, *The Epistle to the Romans*, tr. from the 6th ed. by Edwyn C. Hoskyns (New York: Oxford University Press, 1968). For a study of Barth's ethics, see Robert E. Willis, *The Ethics of Karl Barth* (Leiden: E.J. Brill, 1971).

37. Reinhold Niebuhr, *Moral Man and Immoral Society* (New York: Charles Scribner's Sons, 1932; republished in 1960). For a recent evaluation of Niebuhr, see Ronald H. Stone, *Reinhold Niebuhr: Prophet to Politicians* (New York: Abingdon Press, 1972).

38. Reinhold Niebuhr, *Beyond Tragedy: Essays on the Christian Interpretation of History* (New York: Charles Scribner's Sons, 1937; republished in 1965).

39. As illustrations of this approach, see Harvey Cox, *The Secular City*, and Thomas J.J. Altizer and William Hamilton, *Radical Theology and the Death of God* (Indianapolis: Bobbs-Merrill Company, 1966).

40. *The Secular City Debate*, ed. Daniel Callahan (New York: Macmillan Company, 1966).

41. Johannes B. Metz, *Theology of the World* (New York: Seabury Press, 1973), part one, pp. 13-77. In the preface Metz indicates that the essays in this book were written between 1961 and 1967. Although Metz does not explicitly acknowledge any development in the preface, the reader can readily see the development in the book, with part one representing the incarnational stage. See Francis Fiorenza, "The Thought of J.B. Metz," *Philosophy Today* 10 (1966), 247-252.

42. Metz, "Chapter Three: An Eschatological View of the Church and the World," *Theology of the World*, pp. 81-97.

43. Johannes B. Metz, "The Future in the Memory of Suffering," *New Concilium* 76 (1972), 9-25; Metz, "The Future Ex Memoria Passionis," in *Hope and the Future of Man*, ed. Ewert Cousins (Philadelphia: Fortress Press, 1972), pp. 117-131.

44. Johannes B. Metz, "For a Renewed Church before a Renewed Council: A Concept in Four Theses," in *Towards Vatican III: The Work That Needs to Be Done*, ed. David Tracy with Hans Küng and Johannes B. Metz (New York: Seabury, 1978), pp. 137-145. The suffering and apocalyptic themes are also found in his latest book containing articles published in the 1970s—Johannes Baptist Metz, *Faith in History and Society: Toward a Practical Fundamental Theology* (New York: Seabury, 1980).

PART FOUR

Social Ethics

8. The Changing Anthropological Bases of Catholic Social Ethics

For one hundred years there has existed a body of official Catholic Church teaching on social ethics and the social mission of the church. There was a social teaching within the Catholic Church before that time, but from the pontificate of Leo XIII (1878-1903) one can speak of a body of authoritative social teaching worked out in a systematic way and often presented in the form of encyclicals or papal letters to the bishops and to the whole church. The purpose of this chapter is to point out some of the changing anthropological emphases in this body of social teaching, thereby proposing an approach which can and should be employed in Christian social ethics today. The limitation of our discussion primarily to the official body of papal teaching should not be construed as failing to recognize the other theological approaches within the Catholic community. However, the teaching of the hierarchical. magisterium has a special degree of authority about it and historically has served as a basis for much of Catholic social teaching during the last hundred years. Also by limiting the discussion to this particular body of teaching it is possible to place some realistic perimeters on the study.

Until a few years ago Catholic commentators were generally reluctant to admit any development within the papal social teaching.[1] The popes themselves gave the impression of continuity and even went out of their way to smooth over any differences with their "predecessors of

happy memory." Often Catholic commentaries on the
papal teaching were uncritical—merely explaining and
applying the papal teaching. John F. Cronin, one of the
better known commentators on Catholic social teaching
in the United States, while reminiscing in 1971, recognized his failure to appreciate the historical and cultural
conditionings of this teaching and the importance of a
proper hermeneutic in explaining it.[2] In the area of
church and state relations and religious liberty the
historically and culturally conditioned aspect of the papal
teaching was clearly recognized somewhat earlier.[3] In the
last few years more scholars have realized the development
and change which have occurred in Catholic social
teaching.[4] Especially since the decade of the 1960s this
development has become so pronounced that no one
could deny its existence.

This study will concentrate on anthropology, but it will
be impossible to treat all aspects of anthropology. Two
anthropological aspects will be considered in depth. The
first section on the personal aspects of anthopology will
trace the development culminating in an emphasis on the
freedom, equality, and participation of the person. Some
of the important methodological consequences of such an
understanding of the human person will also be discussed. The second section on the social aspects of
anthropology will show the greater importance given to
the social dimensions of existence especially in terms of
private property and of the approach to socialism.[5]

I. Personal Aspects of Anthropology

Octogesima adveniens, the apostolic letter of Pope Paul
VI written on the occasion of the eightieth anniversary of
Rerum novarum, proposes an anthropology highlighting
the freedom and dignity of the human person which are
seen above all in two aspirations becoming ever-more
prevalent in our world—the aspiration to equality and the
aspiration to participation.[6] Freedom, equality, and participation are the significant characteristics of the anthropology of *Octogesima adveniens.*

The differences with the writings of Leo XIII are striking. The church at the time of Leo was fearful of freedom and equality and looked on the majority of people as the untutored multitude who had to be guided or directed by their rulers.[7]

Pope Leo condemned the "modern liberties." Liberty of worship goes against the "chiefest and holiest human duty" demanding the worship of the one true God in the one true religion which can easily be recognized by its external signs. Liberty of speech and of the press means that nothing will remain sacred, for truth will be obscured by darkness, and error will prevail. There is only a right and a duty to speak what is true and honorable and no right to speak what is false. A like judgment is passed on liberty of teaching. Finally liberty of conscience is considered. The only true meaning of the freedom of conscience is the freedom to follow the will of God and to do one's duty in obeying his commands. At best the public authority can tolerate what is a variance with truth and justice for the sake of avoiding greater evils or of preserving some greater good.[8] Leo XIII was certainly no supporter of civil liberties and the modern freedoms.

Leo XIII not only did not promote equality as a virtue or something to be striven for in society, but he stressed the importance of inequality. Inequality is a fact of nature. There are differences in health, beauty, intelligence, strength, and courage. These natural inequalities necessarily bring about social inequalities which are essential for the good functioning of society. In short, the inequality of rights and of power proceed from the very author of nature. Leo had a view of society as a hierarchical organism in which there are different roles and functions to fulfill, but in which all will work for the common good of all.[9]

According to Leo:

> In like manner, no one doubts that all men are equal one to another, so far as regards their common origin and nature, or the last end which each one has to attain, or the rights and duties which are thence derived. But, as the abilities of all are not equal, as one differs from another in the powers of mind

or body, and as there are many dissimilarities óf manner, disposition and character, it is most repugnant to reason to endeavor to confine all within the same measure, and to extend complete equality to the institutions of civil life.[10]

Inequalities and some of the hardships connected with them will always be part of human existence in a world which is marked by the presence of original sin. To suffer and to endure is the lot of people. People should not be deluded by promises of undisturbed repose and constant enjoyment. We should look upon our world in a spirit of reality and at the same time seek elsewhere the solace to its troubles.[11]

Leo XIII likewise does not call for the active participation of all in social and political life, but rather he has a very hierarchical view of civil society which follows from the inequalities mentioned above. Leo's favorite word for the rulers of society is *principes*. The very word shows his hierarchical leanings. The citizen is primarily one who obeys the divine law, the natural law, and the human law which are handed down by the *principes*. Leo even quotes the maxim *qualis rex, talis grex* (as the King, so the herd— the people), which indicates the power of the ruler over all the citizens in practically every aspect of life.[12] The citizens are called by Leo the untutored multitude who must be led and protected by the ruler.[13] At best, authority appears as paternalistic, and the subjects are children who are to obey and respect their rulers with a type of piety.[14] Leo was fearful of the liberalistic notion of the sovereignty of the people, which really meant that the people no longer owed obedience to God and God's law in all aspects of their public and private lives.[15]

In this authoritarian and paternalistic understanding there is no distinction between society and the state which had been present in classical thought but then lost during the period of absolutism. Leo's theory is that of the ethical society-state in which the total common good of the society is entrusted to the rulers. Society is constructed from the top down with the ruler guarding and protecting the untutored multitude from the many dangers of life just as the father has the function of protecting and guiding his children in the family.[16]

Leo's denial of liberty, equality, and participation can be somewhat understood in the light of the circumstances of the times in which he lived. The pope was an implacable foe of a liberalism which in his mind was the root cause of all the problems of the modern day. Liberalism substitutes foolish license for true liberty. The followers of liberalism deny the existence of any divine authority and proclaim that every human being is a law unto oneself. Liberalism proposes an independent morality in which the human being is freed from the divine law and authority and can do whatever one wants. Leo consequently attacks those forms of government which make the collective reason of the community the supreme guide of life in society. They substitute the decision of the majority for the rule of God. God and God's law are totally removed from society.[17]

Behind Leo's fear of equality lurks the same individualism present in liberalism. For Leo society is an organism. Human beings are by nature social and called to join together in political society for the common good. To live in society is not a restriction on individual human freedom, for by nature all of us are social. Each one has a different function to play in the hierarchically structured organism which resembles the organism of the human body with all its different parts, but each functioning for the good of the whole. Leo fears an understanding which sees society merely as a collection of equal individuals, for this would destroy any social fabric and true social ordering. Participation is also looked on as a threat, for this could readily be confused with the demands of liberalistic license and destroy the organic unity of a society in which each person has one's God-given function to perform. In the context of Leo's understanding of the untutored multitude there could be little or no room for participation.

In general Leo rightly recognized some of the problems of liberalism and individualism. However, his only solution was to turn his back totally on all the developments which were then taking place in the modern world. At the very least Leo lacked the prophetic charisma to sort out the good from the bad in the newer developments which were taking place in the nineteenth century and to find a place for the legitimate demands of liberty, equality, and participation.[18] The picture emerges of a static and hierarchically structured authoritarian society governed by the law of God and the natural law under the protection and guidance of a paternalistic ruler who directs all to the common good and protects his subjects from physical and moral harm.

This explanation of Leo's approach shows the tremendous gulf which exists between his understanding of anthropology and that proposed by Pope Paul VI in *Octogesima adveniens*. However, one can trace some of the major lines of the development which occurred from Leo XIII to Paul VI.

Even in Leo XIII there are some aspects pointing in a different direction, but they are found mostly in his 1891 encyclical *Rerum novarum* on the rights of the worker. In his political writings Leo especially argues against a totalitarian democracy with its emphasis on majority rule and its lack of respect for divine and natural law, but he always upheld the basic rights of individual human beings which might be abused because of the totalitarian democracy. In *Rerum novarum* he stresses even more the rights of the individual worker, and his approach is less authoritarian and paternalistic. In *Rerum novarum* Leo recalls, while pointing out the danger of socialism, that the human being is prior to the state and has natural rights which do not depend on the state.[19] The right to private property is based on our nature as rational and provident beings. Every individual has the right to marry. Marriage is older than the state and has its rights and duties independently of the state.[20] The state has an obligation to intervene to protect the rights of the workers, for public authority must step in when a particular class suffers or is threatened with harm which in no other way can be met or avoided.[21] Moreover, workers themselves have the right to organize into unions and associations to promote their own rights and interests.[22] Here appears the basis for participation in the shaping of one's own destiny.

In *Rerum novarum* Leo repeats his teaching on inequality. The condition of things inherent in human affairs must be borne with. These conditions include natural differences of the most important kinds—differences in capacities, skills, health, and strength. Unequal fortune is a necessary result of unequal conditions.[23] However, Leo appears to admit a basic equality of all to have their rights recognized and protected by the state. In fact the poor and badly off have a claim to special consideration.[24] As one would expect, Leo upholds the rights of the individual against socialism. In tension with his other emphases Leo's writings show differing degrees of recognition of some freedom, equality, and even of incipient participation as anthropological concerns.

Pope Pius XI (1922-1939) remains in continuity with his predecessor Leo XIII. Liberalism lies at the root of the problems of the modern world. The principal cause of the disturbed conditions in which we live is that the power of law and respect for authority have been considerably weakened ever since people came to deny that the origin of law and of authority was in God, the creator and ruler of the world. Liberalism has even fathered socialism and bolshevism. Pius XI insists on the importance of natural law and a hierarchical ordering of society based on it. In *Quadragesimo anno* on the fortieth anniversary of Leo's encyclical *Rerum novarum* Pius XI continues the discussion of justice and the economic order, insisting on the dignity and rights of the individual and also on the social nature of human beings. Here again the two extreme approaches of individualism and socialism are rejected on the basis of an anthropology which recognizes the dignity and rights of the individual as well as the social aspects of the human person.[25]

However, contact with different forms of totalitarianism brought to the fore an emphasis on the defense of the rights, dignity, and freedom of the individual. (There has been much discussion in the last few decades about the relationship of the Catholic Church to facism, nazism, and communism. Without entering into the debate, it is safe to generalize that the Catholic Church was much more fearful of the left and showed itself more willing to compromise with the right.) Pius XI defends the transcendental character of the human person against materialistic and atheistic communism. Communism is condemned for stripping human beings of their liberty and for robbing the human person of dignity.[26] Now the church becomes the protector of human freedom and dignity. In *Non abbiamo bisogno* Pius XI even defends the freedom of conscience with the recognition that he is speaking about the true freedom of conscience and not the license which refuses to recognize the laws of God.[27]

The development continues in the pontificate of Pope Pius XII (1939-1958). The historical context of the struggle against totalitarianism remains, but the significant role of Christian Democratic parties in Europe adds an important new dimension. In his Christmas radio message in 1944 Pope Pius XII insisted on the dignity of human beings and on a system of government that will be more in accord with the dignity and freedom of the citizenry. This emphasis on the dignity and freedom of the human being also calls for greater participation and active involvement of all. The human being is not the object of social life or an inert element in it, but rather is the subject, foundation, and end of social life.[28]

In the light of these historical circumstances and of a theoretical insistence on the centrality of the dignity of the human person, Pius proposed an understanding of the state remarkably different from that of Leo XIII. As John Courtney Murray lucidly points out, Pius XII abandoned Leo XIII's ethical concept of the society-state and accepted a juridical or limited constitutional state. For Leo there is no distinction between society and the state, for the state is hierarchically ordered, with the rulers having the function of guarding and protecting the illiterate masses in every aspect of life. By emphasizing the dignity, freedom, and responsibility of the individual person Pius XII clearly accepts a limited view of the state which sees it as only a part of society with a function of defending the rights of human beings and of promoting the freedom of the people. The state has a limited juridical role and does not act as the parent who guides the entire lives of one's children. No longer is the state understood in terms of the relationship between *principes* and the untutored multitudes. The rulers are representatives of the people, and the people are responsible citizens.[29]

Despite these significant changes in the importance of the dignity of the person and the recognition of limited constitutional government, Guzzetti still detects an air of the aristocratic about Pius XII's approach.[30] Also on the matter of inequalities in society Pius advances over Leo, but still insists that natural inequalities of education, of earthly goods, and of social position are not obstacles to brotherhood and community provided they are not arbitrary and are in accord with justice and charity.[31]

The short pontificate of John XXIII (1958-1963) with its convocation of the Second Vatican Council had a great impact on Roman Catholicism. In the area of social ethics John in his two encyclicals *Mater et magistra* and *Pacem in terris* defends human dignity in the midst of the ever-increasing social relationships and interdependencies which characterize our modern world. *Pacem in terris* gives the most detailed statement in the papal social tradition of human rights based on the dignity of the person but also adds the corresponding duties, thereby avoiding the danger of individualism. The dignity of the human person requires that every individual enjoy the right to act freely and responsibly. The dignity, freedom, and equality of the human person are highlighted and defended, but many of the assumptions of an older liberalistic individualism are not accepted.[32]

There is one fascinating development even within John's own writings. The papal social tradition consistently emphasized that life in society must be based on truth, justice, and love. John XXIII repeated the importance of this triad in *Mater et magistra* in 1961.[33] However, in 1963 in *Pacem in terris* a fourth element was added: a political society is well ordered, beneficial, and in keeping with human dignity if is grounded on truth, justice, love, and freedom.[34] Even in John there was only a later recognition of the fundamental importance of freedom alongside truth, justice, and love.

From the first encyclical of Leo XIII on the question of economic ethics there was some recognition for participation and responsibility, especially in terms of the workers' right to form organizations and unions to promote their own interests. John XXIII recognizes there is an innate need of human nature calling for human beings engaged in productive activity to have an opportunity to assume responsibility and to perfect themselves by their efforts. Participation of workers in medium-size and larger enterprises calls for some type of partnership.[35]

Two documents of the Second Vatican Council are most significant for our purposes—the Declaration on Religious Freedom and the Pastoral Constitution on the Church in the Modern World. It was only at the Second Vatican Council that the Roman Catholic Church accepted the concept of religious liberty—a concept which was anathema to Leo XIII. However, the council is careful to show that its acceptance does not stem from the tenets of an older liberalism and indifferentism. Religious liberty is the right, not to worship God as one pleases, but rather the right to immunity from external coercion forcing one to act in a way opposed to one's conscience or preventing one from acting in accord with one's conscience. The basis for religious liberty is stated very distinctly in the opening paragraph—the dignity of the human person which has been impressing itself more and more deeply on the conscience of contemporary people and a corresponding recognition of a constitutional government whose powers are limited. A limited government embraces only a small part of the life of people in society, and religion exists beyond the pale of the role of civil government.[36] The council brings out all the implications of a limited constitutional government which in principle had been accepted by Pius XII. The Roman Catholic Church thus became a defender of religious liberty even though in the nineteenth century the papacy stood as the most determined opponent of religious liberty.

The dignity of the human person serves as the cornerstone of the Pastoral Constitution on the Church in the Modern World—*Gaudium et spes*. The first chapter of the theoretical part one of the document begins with the dignity of the human person and its meaning and importance. Authentic freedom as opposed to license is championed by the conciliar document. In earlier documents there was a great insistence on the moral law as the antidote to any tendency to license. Now the emphasis is on conscience—the most secret core and sanctuary of the human person where one hears the call of God's voice. The shift from the role of law, which is traditionally called the objective norm of morality, to conscience, which is called the subjective norm of human action, is most significant in showing the move to the subject and to the person. Of course the document stresses the need for a correct conscience, but the impression is given that truth is found in the innermost depth of one's existence.[37]

Gaudium et spes gives much more importance to equality than some of the earlier documents. Inequalities are still recognized, but now the existence of inequalities appears in subordinate clauses with the main emphasis being on equality. For example: "True, all men are not alike from the point of view of varying physical power and the diversity of intellectual and moral resources. Nevertheless, with respect to the fundamental rights of the person, every type of discrimination, whether social or cultural, whether based on sex, race, color, social condition, language or religion, is to be overcome and eradicated as contrary to God's intent.[38] "Moreover although rightful differences exist between men, the equal dignity of persons demands that a more humane and just condition of life be brought about. For excessive economic and social differences between the members of the one human family or population groups cause scandal, and militate against social justice, equity, the dignity of the human person as well as social and international peace."[39]

There is also a call for responsibility and participation. The will to play one's role in common endeavors should be encouraged. The largest possible number of citizens should participate in public affairs with genuine freedom.[40] A greater share in education and culture is required for all to exercise responsibility and participation. The active participation of all in running the economic enterprise should be promoted.[41] The juridical and political structure should afford all citizens the chance to participate freely and actively in establishing the constitutional basis of a political community, governing the state, determining the scope and purposes of different institutions, and choosing leaders.[42]

In the light of this line of development the teaching of Pope Paul VI in *Octogesima adveniens* on the eightieth anniversary of *Rerum novarum* does not come as a total surprise: "Two aspirations persistently make themselves felt in these new contexts, and they grow stronger to the extent that people become better informed and better educated: the aspiration to equality and the aspiration to participation, two forms of man's dignity and freedom."[43] Such an anthropology stressing freedom, equality, and participation should have significant methodological consequences for Christian social ethics.

Historical consciousness

Before considering the methodological consequence of this new anthropology, historical consciousness, which affects both anthropology and methodology, should be considered. Historical consciousness, which is very pronounced in *Octogesima adveniens* but clearly absent from the documents of Leo XIII, gives great significance to historical conditions, growth, change, and development, and has often been contrasted with a classicist approach. In the area of methodology the classicist approach emphasizes the eternal, the universal, and the unchanging, and often employs a deductive methodology. The historically conscious approach emphasizes the particular, the individual, the contingent, and the historical, and often employs a more inductive methodology.[44]

The importance of historical consciousness becomes very evident in the deliberations of the Second Vatican Council on religious freedom. Pope Leo XIII had condemned religious liberty. Perhaps the most pressing question facing the fathers of Vatican II was how to reconcile Leo's condemnation with the acceptance of religious liberty less than a century later. John Courtney Murray in his writings on religious liberty provided a solution. One has to interpret Leo in the light of the circumstances of his own day. Leo was struggling against a Continental liberalism with its denial of any place for God in society and its acceptance of an omnicompetent state with no recognition whatsoever of the divine law or of natural law. In reaction to this approach Leo called for the union of church and state as the way rightfully recognizing and protecting the role and function of the church. However, the constitutional understanding of separation of church and state was based, not on a Continental liberalism, but on a notion of a constitutional government which claimed only a limited role for itself in the life of society. The constitutional understanding did not deny a role or a place for religion in society; the role and function of religion existed beyond the pale of the limited scope and function of the state. Murray's historically conscious hermeneutic distinguished the polemical-historical aspect of Leo's teaching from the doctrinal aspect. There has been no change in the doctrinal. The recognition of historical consciousness provided the key to the problem of development and change in the church's teaching.[45] Murray made a remarkable contribution by his historical hermeneutic. In retrospect it is both easy and necessary to criticize Murray's theory as too benevolent. One should admit some error in the church's teaching in the nineteenth century and even some doctrinal discontinuity and evolution in the teaching on religious liberty.

The acceptance of historical consciousness in our understanding of anthropology also has important methodological ramifications in the papal social teaching. The earlier teachings were deductive, stressing immutable eternal principles of natural law. However, a more inductive approach began to appear in the 1960s. The encyclical *Pacem in terris* is divided into four major parts: order among people, relations between individuals and

public authority within a single state, relations between
states, relations of people in political communities with
the world community. Each part concludes with a section
on the signs of the times—the distinctive characteristics of
the contemporary age.[46] There was much debate about the
term "signs of the times" at the Second Vatican Council.
Early drafts and versions of the Constitution on the
Church in the Modern World gave great importance to the
term. In the final version "signs of the times" was used
sparingly because some council fathers did not want to use
a term whose biblical meaning was quite different—the
eschatological signs of the last days.[47] However, in the
second part of the Pastoral Constitution which treats five
problems of special urgency in the contemporary world,
each consideration begins with an empirical description
of the contemporary reality even though the terminology
"signs of the times" is not employed. Such an approach
gives greater emphasis to the contemporary historical
situation and does not begin with a universal viewpoint
and deduce an understanding applicable to all cultures
and times.

Methodological consequences

The anthropology of the papal social teaching by the
time of *Octogesima adveniens* in 1971 stresses freedom,
equality, participation, and historical mindedness. The
methodological consequences of such an anthropology
are quite significant and show a remarkable change from
the methodology employed in the earlier documents. The
earlier approach highlighted the universal, all-embracing
character of the teaching. In retrospect, however, the
claimed universalism of the earlier encyclicals was really
limited to European socioeconomic conditions. In the
economic realm there appeared especially with Pius XI in
1931 a plan for the reconstruction of the social order in
accord with what was called a theory of moderate solidar-
ism. Pope Pius XI was much more negative about the
existing abuses and injustices of the social order than was
Leo XIII. Undoubtedly the problem of the depression

influenced Pius's negative judgment about the existing social order and the call for a more radical reconstruction of society according to a solidaristic model based in general on the guild system with its intermediary institutions bringing together both workers and owners. The pope continued to condemn laissez-faire capitalism and the opposite extreme of socialism. In place of these two systems Pius XI proposed a third way which would eliminate the bad features of extreme individualism and extreme socialism while giving due importance to the personal and social nature of the individual person. This third way, although somewhat vague in its development and detail, was thought to be a universally applicable plan.[48]

Pius XII continued in the same line as his predecessor with an emphasis on reconstruction and not merely on reform. Professional organizations and labor unions are provisional and transitory forms; the ultimate purpose is the bringing together and cooperation of employees and employers in order to provide together for the general welfare and the needs of the whole community. Pope Pius XII also distinguished his reconstruction plan from mere comanagement, or participation of workers in management. Pope Pius XII originally followed the footsteps of his predecessor in proposing a universally applicable plan of reconstruction deduced from the principles of the natural law and corresponding in significant ways to the guild system of the middle ages. However, after 1952 Pius rarely mentioned such a plan of reconstruction.[49] In *Mater et magistra* Pope John XXIII merely referred to Pius XI's orderly reorganization of society with smaller professional and economic groups existing in their own right and not prescribed by public authority.[50] In John's encyclicals, in the conciliar documents, and in Paul's teaching there was no further development of Pius XI's plan for social reconstruction.

Reasons for the abandonment of a plan of social reconstruction applicable throughout the world can be found in the later documents themselves. These documents recognize the complexity of the social problem and

historical and cultural differences which make it difficult
for a universal plan to be carried out in all different areas.
Mater et magistra emphasized the complexity of the
present scene, the multiplication of social relationships,
and many new developments in the field of science,
technology, and economics as well as developments in the
social and political fields.[51] The social questions involve
more than the rights and duties of labor and captital. In
Populorum progressio Pope Paul VI early in his encyclical stated that today the principal fact that all must
recognize is that the social question has become world-
wide.[52] The complexity of the question increases enor-
mously when one brings into consideration the entire
world and the relationship between and among countries,
especially poor nations and rich nations. The approach of
the Pastoral Constitution on the Church in the Modern
World by beginning with the signs of the times also called
for doing away with a deductive methodology resulting in
an eternal, immutable plan of God for the world.

At the same time as Pius XI and Pius XII were talking
about a program of reconstruction according to solidaristic principles of organization, the term "social doctrine"
was used by these popes to refer to the official body of
church teaching consisting of the principles of the
economic order derived from the natural law and the plan
of reconstruction based on them. Pius XI distinguished
this social doctrine from social and economic sciences.
The social doctrine contains the immutable truths taught
by the popes, whereas social science is the area for research
and scholarly enterprise. Precisely the authoritative nature of the doctrine distinguishes it from the empirical
social sciences of economics or sociology.[53] Such an
approach was called for by some Catholic sociologists
who claimed that the major of their argument was
supplied by authoritative church teaching, the minor
came from their scientific research, and from these one
drew the conclusion.[54] Pope Pius XII frequently speaks
about Catholic social doctrine. According to Pius XII the
earlier papal teaching became the source of Catholic
social doctrine by providing the children of the church

with directives and means for a social reconstruction rich in fruit.[55] Social doctrine is the authoritative teaching proclaimed by the hierarchical magisterium, deduced from the eternal principles of the natural law, and distinguished from the contribution of the empirical sciences.

Both the term "social doctrine of the church" and the reality expressed by it—namely, a papal plan or ideology of social reconstruction—gradually disappear from official church documents after Pope Pius XII. Later references are to the social teaching of the gospel or the social teaching of the church. Gone is the vision of the universal plan deductively derived from natural law and proposed authoritatively by the church magisterium to be applied in all parts of the world. No longer will there be such a separation between ethically deduced moral principles and the economic and social analysis of the situation. Rather, one now begins with the signs of the times and with an analysis of the contemporary situation and not with some abstract principle divorced from historical reality.[56]

Octogesima adveniens with an anthropology insisting on personal freedom, equality, participation, and historical consciousness employs a methodology quite at variance with that employed in the early papal documents. Early in the document Pope Paul VI recognizes the wide diversity of situations in which Christians live throughout the world. In the face of such diversity it is difficult to utter a unified message or to put forward a solution which has universal validity. The Christian communities themselves must analyze with objectivity their own situation and shed on it the light of the gospel and the principles of the teaching of the church. It is up to the Christian communities with the help of the Spirit in communion with the bishops and in dialogue with other Christians and people of good will to discern the options and commitments necessary to bring about the urgently needed social and political changes.[57] Rather than a universal plan based on natural law, Pope Paul VI recalls the importance and significance of utopias. Utopias appeal to the imagination of responsible people to perceive in the present situation the disregarded possibilities within it and to provide direction toward a fresh future. Such an approach sustains social dynamism by the confidence that it gives to the inventive powers of the human mind and heart. "At the heart of the world there dwells the mystery of man discovering himself to be God's son in the course of a historical and psychological process in which constraint and freedom as well as the weight of sin and the breath of the Spirit alternate and struggle for the upper hand."[58]

The methodological changes are quite significant. There is no universal plan applicable to all situations, but rather Christians discern what to do in the midst of the situation in which they find themselves. What to do is not determined by a deductive reasoning process based on the eternal and immutable natural law. Rather, a careful and objective scrutiny of the present reality in the light of the gospel and of the teaching of the church is central to the discernment process. Commitments and options are discerned in the situation itself. The approach is dynamic rather than static. The appeal to utopias, imagination, and the mystery of the human person at the heart of the world all testify to a less rationalistic discernment process. There is also an admonition for the individual in the church to be self-critical, thereby recognizing the dangers that might come from one's own presuppositions.

Octogesima adveniens concludes with a call to action.[59] All along the church's social teaching has called for action, but the call is now more urgent and more central to the very notion of the social mission of the church. The condition of individual responsibility and the urgent need to change structures require the active involvement of all. Once again emphasis is on the need to take concrete action despite the fact that there can be a plurality of strategic options for Christians.

Both the anthropology and the methodology employed in *Octogesima adveniens* outline a different understanding of the role of persons in the church itself and in the social mission of the church. An older approach, especial-

ly associated with the concept of Catholic Action proposed by Pope Pius XI and Pope Pius XII, saw the
function of the laity to carry out and put into practice the
principles which were taught by the hierarchical magisterium. As is evident in this document, the whole church
must discern what options are to be taken in the light of an
analysis of the signs of the times and in the light of the
gospel even though there remains a distinctive role for
hierarchical magisterium. No longer are the laity the
people who receive the principles and the instruction
from the hierarchy and then put these plans into practice.
All in the church have a role in discerning and in
executing.[60]

Contemporary Catholic social ethics mirrors and at
times even goes beyond the approach and methodology
employed in *Octogesima adveniens*. David Hollenbach
has recently employed a similar methodology in his
attempt to revise and retrieve the Catholic human rights
tradition.[61] Political and liberation theologies show some
of the same tendencies but even go beyond the methodological approach of *Octogesima adveniens*. Critical
reason insists on the importance of action. Praxis becomes
primary in many of these approaches, and theology
becomes reflection on praxis. For many liberation theologians, true theology can only grow out of praxis.[62] At
the very least the methodology of Catholic social ethics is
thus greatly changed from the time of Leo XIII, especially
in the light of changing anthropological understandings.

II. Social Aspects of Anthropology

Another important aspect of anthropology concerns the
social nature of human beings. Catholic social ethics has
consistently recognized the social nature of human beings.
As a result Catholic social ethics looks upon the state as a
natural society, for human beings are called by nature to
live in political society. In some Christian ethics the
origin of the state is grounded on human sinfulness. The
power and coercion of the state are necessary to prevent

sinful human beings from destroying one another.[63] Pope
Leo XIII follows in the Catholic tradition by his insistence that the state is a natural society. Human beings
with their inequality and differences come together to
achieve what the individuals as such are not able to
accomplish. Leo's understanding of political society as an
organism and an organic whole with individuals carrying
out different functions shows that the state is based on
human nature and does not exist merely on the basis of a
contract made by discrete individuals.[64]

The papal social teaching in the last century has
recognized both the legitimate rights of the individual and
the social nature of human beings. The Catholic approach to the economic problem traditionally has condemned the two extremes of individualistic capitalism
and collectivistic socialism. Throughout its history Catholic social ethics has tried to uphold both the personal and
the social aspects of anthropology. However, there have
been varying nuances in the approach over the years. This
section of the chapter will now consider two significant
questions in which there has been a development in
giving more importance to the social aspects of anthropology—private property and socialism.

Private property

Pope Leo XIII recognized the misery and wretchedness
pressing so urgently upon the majority of the working
class because of the hard heartedness of employers and the
greed of unchecked competition. To remedy these ills the
socialists do away with private property. However, Leo's
solution is the opposite. Everyone has a right to private
property. The dignity of the individual will be protected if
one is able to have one's own property and thus make
oneself secure against the vicissitudes of the industrial
order. Private property protects and promotes the security
of the individual and of the family. By investing wages in
property and in land the worker has the hope and the
possibility of increasing personal resources and of better-
ing one's condition in life.

However, the most important and fundamental fact for
Leo is that private property is a demand of the natural law.
The human being is distinguished from animals precisely
through rational nature, because of which one has the
right to possess things in a permanent and stable way to
provide for one's own continued existence. The human
individual can only provide for the future through private
property. By virtue of labor and work the human being
makes one's own that portion of nature's field which she
or he cultivates. The principle of private ownership is
necessarily in accord with human nature and is conducive
in the most unmistakable manner to the peace and
tranquility of human existence. The right of the individual to private property is strengthened in the light of
human social and domestic obligations, for it provides
security for the entire family. The first and most fundamental principle to alleviate the impoverished conditions
of the masses is the inviolability of private property.[65]

There are a number of interesting facets about Leo's
defense of private property as the solution to the misery of
the working masses. First, Leo's solution indicates the
rural and preindustrial perspective with which he ap-
proached the problem. Private property for Leo is usually
the land and one's right to the fruits of the labor which has
been expended in cultivating the land. If the individual
possesses one's own land, then one can provide food and
basic necessities for one's family no matter what the
vicissitudes of the industrial order. Human dignity is
preserved and human needs will be met if the workers can
own and work their own plot of land. This solution
obviously fits better in an earlier time and in a more
agrarian situation. Its practicality as a reasonable solution
in the industrial era of the late nineteenth century is open
to serious question.

Second, Leo does not deal realistically with the most
significant aspect of private property existing at that
time—the abuse of private property by the rich at the
expense of the poor. The failure to recognize this fact in
the very first part of the encyclical and to deal with it
realistically marks a definite lacuna in Leo's approach.

The real problem of the day concerned especially the ownership of the goods of production, since abuses on the part of those who own the goods of production contributed greatly to the economic woes of the worker. Leo reminds the rich of their obligation to share with the poor, but such a reminder does not go to the heart of the problem. As mentioned above, Leo supports the rights of workers to organize to secure their rights, but he does not directly address the existing structural abuses of great wealth in the hands of a few at the expense of the vast majority.

Third, and somewhat connected with the two previous observations, Leo justifies private property only on the basis of labor. No other titles are mentioned by Leo in *Rerum novarum* to justify ownership. The single title of labor again shows the rural vision which Leo brought to the question and which does not take into consideration the many problems of abuse through inheritance and other ways of acquiring private property. In *Quod apostolici muneris* Leo held that inheritance was a valid means of aquiring wealth but did not justify this title.[66] Leo's discussion of the titles to private ownership is very incomplete and again fails to deal with the real abuses and problems of the times.

Fourth, Leo's teaching on private property disagrees with that proposed by Thomas Aquinas. Thomas Aquinas discusses the question of private property in two articles.[67] First he responds affirmatively to the question whether the possession of external things is natural to human beings. God created all reality and ordained that the lower creation serve the higher. Dominion over external things is natural to humans because as a rational creature made in the image and likeness of God the human being is called to use external goods to achieve one's end. But then in a second question Thomas discusses the right to possess something as one's own with the power of procuring and disposing of it. Human beings have the right to private ownership which involves the procuring and disposing of external goods. This right is necessary for human life for three reasons: 1) Everyone is more solicitous about procuring things that will belong to the individual alone and not to the community. 2) A more orderly and less confusing existence will result from private property. 3) A more peaceful state of existence ensues when everyone is content with one's own things. However, with regard to the use of private property human beings are to use external goods as though they were common and not proper because these goods should serve the needs of all.

Thomas Aquinas' teaching on private property differs from Leo's on a number of significant points. Thomas clearly distinguishes between a generic dominion that belongs to all human beings to use external things and the specific type of dominion in the system of private property. In Leo's discussion in the beginning of *Rerum novarum* this distinction seems to be almost entirely lacking.[68] In fact, the argument based on rational human nature, which Thomas used to prove the generic dominion of all people over the goods of creation, is employed by Leo to argue for the rights of private property in the strict sense. Thomas' arguments for the right to private property in the strict sense are not really based on human nature as such, but, rather, the three arguments given are all grounded in the existence of human sinfulness. If it were not for human sinfulness, there would be no need for private property in the strict sense. Elsewhere Thomas maintains that in the state of innocence there would be no need for the strict right of private property.[69] Thomas makes the right to private property in the strict sense instrumental and sees it in the light of the more general right of all human beings to the use of external goods.

Later on in his encyclical Leo does recognize the social aspect of property and the fact that the use of private property is to be common in accord with Aquinas' teaching. From this communal use of property he derives the duty of charity, not of justice except in extreme cases, to give one's superfluous goods to the poor. Leo's differences with Aquinas' teaching on private property seem to come primarily from what was introduced into the scholastic tradition by Taparelli d'Azeglio in the nineteenth century.[70]

It is interesting to note that John A. Ryan, the major figure in Catholic social ethics in the United States in the first half of the twentieth century, proposed an instrumental understanding of the right to private property understood in the strict sense. Ryan's argument makes explicit some of Thomas' presuppositions and clarifies the whole meaning of an instrumental understanding of private property. For Ryan, who considers the question primarily in terms of the ownership of land, the first thing to be said about the goods of creation is that they exist to serve the needs of all human beings. Ryan accepts private ownership in the strict sense as what he calls a natural right of the third class. A right of the first class has as its object that which is an intrinsic good, such as the right to life. A right of the second class has as its object that which is directly necessary for the individual, such as the right to marry. A right of the third class has as its object, not what is directly necessary for the individual, but what is indirectly necessary for the individual because it is necessary as a social institution providing for the general welfare. Private ownership in the strict sense provides better for the general social welfare than any other institutional arrangement about the distribution of property. This necessity is proved empirically and inductively. If socialism or some other system would better serve the general welfare, it should be adopted.[71] Ryan's position with its clear and careful relativization of the right to private property in the strict sense would find an echo in the later papal social teaching.

In *Quadragesimo anno* Pius XI gave more stress to the social function of property. He notes the right to private property exists not only so that individuals may provide for themselves and their families but also so that the goods of creation which are destined by the creator for the entire family of humankind may serve their God-given purpose.[72] However, precisely how private property accomplishes this purpose is not developed. In addition, Pope Pius XI neatly covers one of Leo's lacunae in *Rerum novarum* by asserting that ownership is acquired both by labor and by occupancy of something not owned by anyone, as the tradition of all ages as well as the teaching of his predecessor Pope Leo clearly states.[73] No footnote or reference is made to where Leo makes that statement about occupancy.

There was some evolution in the teaching of Pius XII and later in John XXIII. John recognized the realities of the modern industrial society and the importance of professional skill, education, and social insurance and security as ways of protecting the dignity of the individual worker. However, he hastens to add that despite all these modern developments the right of private property including that pertaining to goods devoted to productive enterprises is permanently valid.[74] It appears there is still a tendency to give absolute rather than relative or instrumental value to the right of private property understood in the strict sense.[75]

Gaudium et spes and *Populorum progressio* made more clear the distinction between the generic right of dominion which belongs to all human beings and the right to private property in the strict sense. *Gaudium et spes* begins with the recognition that the goods of creation exist to serve the needs of all. All have a right to a share of earthly goods sufficient for oneself and one's family. Whatever forms of ownership might be, attention must always be paid to the universal purpose for which created goods exist.[76] After affirming the principle of the universal destiny of the goods of creation, *Populorum progressio* maintains that all other rights including that of private property and free commerce are to be subordinated to this principle.[77] Here we have the same teaching as that proposed earlier by John A Ryan. All must admit that in the course of one hundred years the official Catholic teaching has relativized the right to private property in the strict sense and called attention to the need to judge all property institutions in accord with the universal destiny of the goods of creation to serve the needs of all.

Socialism

There has also been a change in the attitude of the papal teaching to socialism. Pope Leo XIII in the first year of his pontificate issued the encyclical *Quod apostolici muneris,* which pointed out the errors of "that sect of men who, under various and almost barbarous names, are called socialists, communists or nihilists."[78] These people deny the supernatural, the plan of God, God's law, and the role of the church. They assert the basic equality of all human beings and deny that respect is due to majesty and obedience to law. They support a revolutionary doctrine, oppose the indissolubility of marriage, and deny the natural-law right of private property. In *Rerum novarum* in 1891 Pope Leo XIII returned in a somewhat systematic way to a discussion of socialism and considered especially its denial of the right of private property, a denial which is against the law of God and of human nature. However, Leo overemphasized the strength of socialism and its force as a world-wide conspiracy. Also he failed to recognize the moderate strands of socialism which were then existing in many parts of the world.[79]

Pope Pius XI in 1931 in *Quadragesimo anno* recognized the differences existing between a more violent socialism called communism and a more moderate form of social-ism which rejects violence and modifies to some degree, if it does not reject entirely, the class struggle and the abolition of private ownership. Obviously communism with its unrelenting class warfare and absolute extermin-ation of private ownership stands condemned. But what about a moderate socialism which has tempered and modified its positions? Has it ceased to be contradictory to the Christian religion? "Whether considered as a doctrine, or an historical fact, or a movement, Socialism, if it remains truly Socialism, even after it has yielded to truth and justice on the points which we have mentioned cannot be reconciled with the teaching of the Catholic Church because its concept of society itself is utterly foreign to Christian truth."[80] Socialism like all errors contains some truths, but its theory of human society is irreconcilable with true Christianity.[81] However, in his portrayal of moderate socialism he wrongly seems to characterize such socialism as sacrificing the higher goods of human beings to the most efficient way of producing external goods.[82] In the 1930s Pope Pius XI concentrated most of his attacks on communism as seen in his later encyclical *Divini redemptoris* of March 19, 1937.

In other parts of the Catholic world there was even a greater recognition of the changes in moderate socialism. The British hierarchy made it clear that the Labor Party in Britain was not condemned for Catholics.[83] In the United States John A. Ryan, while acknowledging the teaching and practical conclusion of Pius XI, pointed out there were only two questionable planks in the 1932 political platform of the American Socialist Party, and even these could be interpreted in conformity with Catholic principles.[84]

In the aftermath of the Second World War the rise of communism led to the cold war in which the Roman Catholic Church stood squarely against communism. Roman Catholicism underwent persecution in communist countries in Eastern Europe. However, a thaw began with the pontificate of Pope John XXIII in 1958, under whose reign there emerged what was often called "the opening to the left." In *Pacem in terris*, without directly referring to communism, John pointed out the need to distinguish between false philosophical teachings on the nature, origin, and destiny of human beings in the universe and the historical movements which were originally based on these teachings. The historical movements are subject to change and evolving historical circumstances. In addition these movements contain some elements that are positive and deserving of approval. Work in common might be possible to achieve economic, social, political, and cultural ends. Great prudence, however, is required in these common enterprises. "It can happen, then, that meetings for the attainment of some practical end, which formerly were deemed inopportune or unproductive, might now or in the future be considered opportune and useful."[85]

Pope Paul VI in *Octogesima adveniens* built on, made explicit, and carried further the distinction between philosophical teaching and historical movements proposed by John XXIII. Both a liberal and a socialist ideology exist, but there are also historical movements.

There are different kinds of expressions of socialism—a generous aspiration and seeking for a more just society, historical movements with a political organization and aim, and an ideology which claims to give a complete and self-sufficient picture of human beings. Marxism also operates at various levels of expression: 1) Marxism as the practice of class struggle, 2) the collective union of political and economic power under the direction of a single party, 3) a socialist ideology based on an historical materialism, 4) a rigorous scientific method of examining social and political realities. While recognizing all these different levels of expression, it would be illusory to forget the link which binds them together. The document then describes the liberal ideology with its erroneous affirmation of the autonomy of the individual.[86]

In the midst of these encounters with the various ideologies the Christian must discern what is to be done. "Going beyond every system, without however failing to commit himself concretely to serving his brothers, he will assert, in the very midst of his options, the specific character of the Christian contribution for a positive transformation of society."[87] This presentation is remarkable in many ways. Both the liberal and Marxist ideology as complete and self-sufficient positions on human nature and destiny are rejected. However, with due prudence and discretion one could opt for a Marxist analysis of social reality provided that one recognizes the danger of its connection with Marxist ideology. As mentioned in the first part of this chapter, the church's teaching is not proposed as a third approach. There is no mention of the social doctrine of the church but rather only the principles which help one to discern the concrete options that are to be taken. The option of a Marxist sociological tool is open to the Christian provided that one recognizes the danger and does not become imprisoned in an ideology. This marks the greatest openness in a papal statement to the Marxist position.

The development in the understanding of Marxism and socialism in the papal documents did not take place in an historical vacuum. In the 1960s discussions between

Christians and Marxists began. Once Christian theology gave greater importance to eschatology and the relationship between the kingdom of God and this world, there was ample room for dialogue with Marxists about improving the lot and condition of human beings in their earthly existence. Christian theologians also recognized that the Marxist's critique of religion as the opiate of the people called for a response. Political theology as a fundamental theology examining the context of revelation called for a deprivatization of theology and a greater emphasis on the political and social dimension of human existence and of theology. Especially in Latin America some Catholics struggling for social change on the practical side found themselves working hand in hand with Marxists for particular social goals. The 1979 meeting of the Latin American Bishops Conference at Puebla has revealed some of the tensions connected with liberation theology and Marxism in South America. Groups of Christians for Socialism began forming in Latin America in the 1970s. But with the return of more repressive regimes these groups have often been scattered. However, in Europe there are small but apparently significant groups of Christians for Socialism.[88]

Meanwhile changes also occurred in Marxism. The differences between Russian and Chinese Marxism became evident as did differences between Moscow and the Eastern European countries. In theory some Marxists called for a humanistic Marxism which gives more importance to the person and also recognizes the importance of the participation of the person in deciding one's future. Eurocommunism also flourished for a while but now seems to have become less important. In these contexts both in theory and in practice some Christians have been trying to discern how they could cooperate with Marxists and even share some of their approaches, especially in terms of sociological analysis of the ills of society.[89] However, many Catholics still remain opposed to any socialist option.

This study has attempted to trace significant developments in the anthropology present in Catholic social

ethics. Significant changes have occurred in the personal
aspects of anthropology culminating in an emphasis on
freedom, equality, participation, and historical mindedness. At the same time the social aspects of anthropology
have been stressed as illustrated in the changing attitudes
toward private property and socialism. In a sense the
perennial challenge of social ethics is to do justice to both
the personal and the social aspects of anthropology.
However, this challenge now exists in a new context.
Christian social ethics building on the present developments must strive to respond to that demand of recognizing the social aspects of human existence and at the same
time highlighting the freedom, equality, and participation of all within an historically conscious perspective.

NOTES

1. For the best commentary available in English, see Jean-
Yves Calvez and Jacques Perrin, *The Church and Social Justice:
The Social Teaching of the Popes from Leo XIII to Pius XII,
1878-1958* (Chicago: Henry Regnery Co., 1961); also Jean-Yves
Calvez, *The Social Thought of John XXIII* (Chicago: Henry
Regnery Co., 1964).

2. John F. Cronin, "Forty Years Later: Reflections and
Reminiscences," *American Ecclesiastical Review* 164 (1971),
310-318. For Cronin's major contribution in the field, see John
F. Cronin, *Social Principles and Economic Life*, rev. ed.
(Milwaukee: Bruce Publishing Co., 1964).

3. The most significant contribution to an understanding of
development in the papal teaching on religious liberty was
made by John Courtney Murray. For a summary of his
approach, see John Courtney Murray, *The Problem of Religious Freedom* (Westminster, Md.: Newman Press, 1965). This
small volume originally appeared as a long article in *Theological Studies* 25 (1964), 503-575.

4. For the best study of development in the papal teaching on
economic questions before the Second Vatican Council, see

Richard L. Camp, *The Papal Ideology of Social Reform: A Study in Historical Development, 1878-1967* (Leiden: E.J. Brill, 1969). For other helpful studies showing development in Catholic social ethics, see Marie Dominique Chenu, *La dottrina sociale della Chiesa: origine e sviluppo, 1891-1971* (Brescia: Editrice Queriniana, 1977); David Hollenbach, *Claims in Conflict: Retrieving and Renewing the Catholic Human Rights Tradition* (New York: Paulist Press, 1979).

5. One very significant aspect of anthropology which will not be discussed here concerns the relationship between anthropology and eschatology and Christology. Before the Second Vatican Council Catholic social teaching accepted a distinction and at times almost a dichotomy between the natural and the supernatural. Grace, gospel, and the kingdom of God had little or nothing to do with life in the world. Contemporary Catholic social ethics strives to overcome that dichotomy as illustrated in liberation theology. The emphasis now rests on the one history in which God is offering freedom from sin and from all the other forms of oppression in the political, social, and economic orders. In the light of this understanding one can readily see that the social mission of the church is a constitutive dimension of the preaching of the gospel and of the church's mission for the redemption of the human race as was pointed out in *Justice in the World* (n. 6), the document released by the Second General Assembly of the Synod of Bishops, November 30, 1971. For my discussion of this most significant development in Catholic social teaching, see my "Dialogue with Social Ethics: Roman Catholic Social Ethics—Past, Present and Future," in *Catholic Moral Theology in Dialogue,* paperback ed. (Notre Dame, Indiana: University of Notre Dame Press, 1976) pp. 111-149.

6. To facilitate a further study of the papal and church documents, references will be given to readily available English translations. For the documents from the time of Pope John, see *The Gospel of Peace and Justice: Catholic Social Teaching Since Pope John,* ed. Joseph Gremillion (Maryknoll, New York: Orbis Books, 1976). References will include the page number in Gremillion as well as the paragraph numbers of the documents, which generally are the official paragraph numbers found in the original and in all authorized translations. Thus the present reference is: *Octogesima adveniens,* n. 22; Gremil-

lion, p. 496. Another readily available compendium of Catholic Church teaching on social ethics is *Renewing the Face of the Earth: Catholic Documents on Peace, Justice and Liberation*, ed. David J. O'Brien and Thomas A Shannon (Garden City, New York: Doubleday Image Books, 1977).

7. References to the encyclicals of Pope Leo XIII will be to *The Church Speaks to the Modern World: The Social Teachings of Leo XIII*, ed. Etienne Gilson (Garden City, New York: Doubleday Image Books, 1954). Thus the present reference is: *Libertas praestantissimum*, n. 23; Gilson, p. 72.

8. *Libertas praestantissimum*, nn. 19-37; Gilson, pp. 70-79. See also *Immortale Dei*, nn. 31-42; Gilson pp. 174-180.

9. *Quod apostolici muneris*, especially nn. 5, 6; Gilson, pp. 192, 193.

10. *Humanum genus*, n. 26; Gilson, p. 130.

11. *Rerum novarum*, nn. 18, 19; Gilson, pp. 214, 215.

12. Murray, *The Problem of Religious Freedom*, pp. 55, 56.

13. *Libertas praestantissimum*, n. 23; Gilson, p. 72.

14. *Immortale Dei*, n. 5; Gilson, p. 163.

15. *Immortale Dei*, n. 31; Gilson, pp. 174, 175.

16. Murray, *The Problem of Religious Freedom*, pp. 55-57.

17. *Libertas praestantissimum*, n. 15; Gilson, pp. 66, 67.

18. For similar judgment on Leo's approach to liberty, see Fr. Refoulé, "L'Église et les libertés de Léon XIII à Jean XXIII," in *Le supplément* 125 (mai 1978), 243-259.

19. *Rerum novarum*, n. 7; Gilson, pp. 208, 209.

20. *Rerum novarum*, nn. 6-12; Gilson pp. 208-211.

21. *Rerum novarum*, n. 36; Gilson, pp. 224, 225.

22. *Rerum novarum*, nn. 49-51; Gilson, pp. 231-233.

23. *Rerum novarum*, n. 17; Gilson, pp. 213, 214.

24. *Rerum novarum*, n. 37; Gilson, pp. 225, 226. Here I disagree with Camp, who on page 32 of *The Papal Ideology of Social Reform* seems to deny in Leo a basic equality of all before the law.

25. References to the encyclicals of Pope Pius XI will be to *The Church and the Reconstruction of the Modern World: The Social Encyclicals of Pope Pius XI*, ed. Terence P. McLaughlin (Garden City, New York: Doubleday Image Books, 1957). McLaughlin, "Introduction," pp. 6-15.

26. *Divini redemptoris*, n. 10; McLaughlin, pp. 369, 370.

27. For a further explanation of this change in the light of opposition to totalitarianism especially from the left, see G.B. Guzzetti, "L'impegno politico dei cattolici nel magistero pontificio dell'ultimo secolo con particolare riguardo all'ultimo ventennio," *La Scuola Cattolica* 194 (1976), 192-210.

28. Radio message, December 24, 1944; *Acta apostolicae sedis* 37 (1945), 11-12; 22.

29. Murray, *The Problem of Religious Freedom*, pp. 65-67.

30. Guzzetti, "L'impegno politico dei cattolici," p. 202.

31. Radio message, December 24, 1944; *Acta apostolicae sedis* 37 (1945), 14.

32. *Pacem in terris*, nn. 8-34; Gremillion, pp. 203-208. See David Hollenbach, *Claims in Conflict*, pp. 62-69.

33. *Mater et magistra*, n. 212; Gremillion, p. 188.

34. *Pacem in terris*, n. 35; Gremillion, p. 208.

35. *Mater et magistra*, nn. 82-103; Gremillion, pp. 161-165.

36. *Dignitatis humanae*, nn. 1, 2; Gremillion, pp. 337-339.

37. *Gaudium et spes*, nn. 12-22; Gremillion, pp. 252-261.

38. *Gaudium et spes*, n. 29; Gremillion, p. 266.

39. Ibid.

40. *Gaudium et spes*, n. 31; Gremillion, p. 267.

41. *Gaudium et spes*, n. 68; Gremillion, pp. 304, 305.

42. *Gaudium et spes*, n. 75; Gremillion, pp. 310-312.

43. *Octogesima adveniens*, n. 22; Gremillion, p. 496.

44. Bernard Lonergan, "A Transition from a Classicist World View to Historical Mindedness," in *Law for Liberty: The Role of Law in the Church Today*, ed. James E. Biechler (Baltimore: Helicon Press, 1967), pp. 126-133.

45. John Courtney Murray, "Vers une intelligence du développment de la doctrine de l'Église sur la liberté religieuse," in *Vatican II: la liberté religieuse* (Paris: Les Éditions du Cerf, 1967), pp. 11-147; Murray, "Religious Liberty and the Development of Doctrine," *The Catholic World* 204 (February 1967), 277-283.

46. *Pacem in terris*, nn. 39-45, 75-79; 126-129; 142-145; Gremillion, pp. 209-210; 217-218; 227-228; 231-232.

47. Charles Moeller, "Preface and Introductory Statement," in *Commentary on the Documents of Vatican II, V: Pastoral Constitution on the Church in the Modern World*, ed. Herbert Vorgrimler (New York: Herder and Herder, 1969), p. 94.

48. *Quadragesimo anno*, nn. 76-149; McLaughlin, pp. 246-274.

49. Camp, *The Papal Ideology of Social Reform*, pp. 128-135.

50. *Mater et magistra*, n. 37; Gremillion, p. 150.

51. *Mater et magistra*, nn. 46-60; Gremillion, pp. 152-156.

52. *Populorum progressio*, n. 3; Gremillion, p. 388.

53. *Quadragesimo anno*, nn. 17-22; McLaughlin, pp. 224, 225.

54. Paul Hanly Furfey, *Fire on the Earth* (New York: Macmillan, 1936), p. 8.

55. Calvez and Perrin, *The Church and Social Justice*, p. 3.

56. Bartolomeo Sorge, "E superato il concetto tradizionale di dottrina sociale della Chiesa?" *La civiltà cattolica* 119 (1968), I, 423-436. However, I disagree with the assignment of roles which Sorge gives to the hierarchical magisterium and the laity. See also Sorge, "L'apporto dottrinale della lettera apostolica 'Octogesima Adveniens'," *La civiltà cattolica* 122 (1971), 417-428.

57. *Octogesima adveniens*, n. 4; Gremillion, p. 487.

58. *Octogesima adveniens*, n. 37; Gremillion, p. 502.

59. *Octogesima adveniens*, nn. 48-52; Gremillion, pp. 509-511.

60. The understanding of eschatology mentioned in footnote 5 which tends to overcome the dichotomy between the supernatural and the natural and the church and the world also influences the position taken here. For a refutation of a distinction of planes approach in the social mission of the church, see Gustavo Gutierrez, *A Theology of Liberation* (Maryknoll, New York: Orbis Press, 1973), pp. 53-58. For an approach which still tends to distinguish too much between the teaching role of the hierarchy and the executing role of the laity, see the articles of Sorge mentioned in footnote 56.

61. David Hollenbach, *Claims in Conflict*.

62. Gutierrez, *A Theology of Liberation;* Juan Luis Segundo, *The Liberation of Theology* (Maryknoll, New York: Orbis Books, 1976).

63. For an authoritative study, see Heinrich A Rommen, *The State in Catholic Thought* (St. Louis: B. Herder, 1945).

64. Gilson, pp. 11-15.

65. *Rerum novarum*, nn. 5-15; Gilson, pp. 207-213.

66. *Quod apostolici muneris*, n. 1; Gilson, p. 190.

67. Thomas Aquinas, *Summa theologiae*, II*a*-II*ae*, q. 66, a. 1 and 2.

68. For an interpretation which sees Leo in greater continuity with Aquinas, see Calvez and Perrin, *The Church and Social Justice*, pp. 259-268.

69. *Summa theologiae*, I*a*, q. 98, a. 1 ad 3.

70. Léon de Sousberghe, "Propriété, 'de droit naturel.' Thèse néoscholastique et tradition scholastique," *Nouvelle revue théologique* 72 (1950), 582-596. See also Camp, *The Papal Ideology of Social Reform*, pp. 55, 56.

71. John A. Ryan, *Distributive Justice* (New York: Macmillan, 1916), pp. 56-60; Reginald G. Bender, "The Doctrine of Private Property in the Writings of Monsignor John A. Ryan," (S.T.D. diss., The Catholic University of American, 1973).

72. *Quadragesimo anno*, n. 45; McLaughlin, p. 234.

73. *Quadragesimo anno*, n. 52; McLaughlin, p. 237.

74. *Mater et magistra*, nn. 104-109; *Pacem in terris*, n. 21; Gremillion, pp. 165, 166; 205.

75. Here and in the following paragraphs I am basically following the analysis of J. Diez-Alegria, "La lettura del magistero pontificio in materia sociale alla luce del suo sviluppo storico," in *Magistero e morale; atti del 3º congresso nazionale dei moralisti* (Bologna: Edizioni Dehoniane, 1970), pp. 211-256. For an analysis which disagrees with some of Diez-Alegria's conclusions, especially his denial of the contemporary validity of an approach based on common use and private possession, but which agrees with the material proposed here, see Angelo Marchesi, "Il pensiero di S. Tommaso d'Aquino e delle enciclice sociali dei papi sul tema della proprietà privata in una recente analisi di P. Diez-Alegria," *Rivista di filosofia neo-scolastico* 62 (1970), 334-344.

76. *Gaudium et spes*, n. 69; Gremillion, p. 305. For an in-depth analysis of the teaching of *Gaudium et spes* on the distribution of the goods of creation, see E. Lio, *Morale e beni terreni: la destinazione universale dei beni terreni nella Gaudium et spes* (Rome: Città Nuova, 1976).

77. *Populorum progressio*, n. 22; Gremillion, p. 394.

78. *Quod apostolici muneris*, n. 1; Gilson, p. 189.

79. Camp, *The Papal Ideology of Social Reform*, pp. 56, 57.

80. *Quadragesimo anno*, n. 117; McLaughlin, p. 260.

81. *Quadragesimo anno*, n. 120; McLaughlin, p. 261.

82. *Quadragesimo anno*, n. 119; McLaughlin, p. 260.

83. Peter Coman, "English Catholics and the Social Order," *Ampleforth Journal* 81 (1976), 47-57.

84. John A. Ryan, *A Better Economic Order* (New York: Harper and Brothers, 1935), pp. 133, 134.

85. *Pacem in terris*, nn. 159, 160; Gremillion, pp. 235, 236.

86. *Octogesima adveniens*, nn. 26-35; Gremillion, pp. 498-501.

87. *Octogesima adveniens*, n. 36; Gremillion, p. 501.

88. Peter Hebblethwaite, *The Christian-Marxist Dialogue: Beginnings, Present Status and Beyond* (New York: Paulist Press, 1977).

89. For an attempt to show that Christianity is compatible with a humanistic socialist option, see Gregory Baum, *The Social Imperative* (New York: Paulist Press, 1979), especially pp. 184-202.

9. Religion, Law, and Public Policy in America

The role of religion in American public life has been a perennial question in the American political ethos. The First Amendment of the Constitution prohibits the establishment of any religion and guarantees the free exercise of religion. Throughout the years there have been different topics that have been discussed in relation to this role of religion. A continuing topic of debate is the question of aid to parochial schools. The purpose of this chapter is to investigate two particular contemporary aspects of the question—the controversies over abortion and over the political involvement of some conservative Christians through groups such as the Moral Majority. In the process, criteria and principles will be proposed to govern the role of religion and of church groups in establishing legislation and public policy. The perspective throughout this chapter is that of a Catholic theologian proposing a criterion for the involvement of faith and religion which should be acceptable to all Americans.

I. Abortion Legislation and the Criterion of Political Purpose

The abortion controversy has raised a number of significant issues in the last few years—the morality of abortion, the legality of abortion, the public funding of abortion. Lawyers, courts, philosophers, theologians, churches, and the general public have been discussing all these issues. This chapter addresses a fourth related question—the issue of religious-motivated and church involvement in seeking and lobbying for particular legislation. The specific question has been raised by the contention of the brief for the plaintiffs in *McRae* v. *Califano* that the Hyde Amendment restricting Medicaid funding for abortion violates the nonestablishment clause of the First Amendment by enacting a particular religious view of abortion into law and because the passage of such legislation resulted from religious influence and lobbying, especially by the Roman Catholic Church.[1] Such reasoning has been rejected by both Judge Dooling in his decision in the United States District Court in New York, which declared that the Hyde Amendment is unconstitutional on other grounds, and by the Supreme Court, which recently decided that the Hyde Amendment is constitutional.[2] However, the issue as such remains important and significant for our country at large and for those interested in the role of religion and of faith in our religiously pluralistic society.

My perspective in this study is not that of a lawyer but of a Catholic theologian. It seems, at least to this nonlawyer, there exists general agreement among lawyers in discussing questions of the establishment clause of the First Amendment in the light of the criteria proposed by the Supreme Court in the Nyquist case (which dealt with aid to private schools): "To pass muster under the Establishment Clause the law in question, first, must reflect a clearly secular legislative purpose . . . second, must have a primary effect that neither advances nor inhibits religion . . . and third, must avoid excessive government entanglement with religion."[3] Lawyers for both the plaintiffs and the defendants in the *McRae* case argue on the basis of these criteria. My perspective must recognize and accept such legal criteria, but I want to analyze the problem precisely from the angle of faith and religion in American public life and to propose the criterion to govern the involvement of churches and of religion in general.

The question has been proposed in terms of functionally distinguishing between the religious and nonreligious purpose in civil law. I would prefer to rephrase the question: How do we determine if the purpose of the law is truly political? I prefer the term "political" to the term "secular" which is now accepted and used by the courts.

The problem centers around the understanding and the definition of religion. It seems all must admit there are two different ways of understanding religion in this context—a narrow and restricted view and a broader understanding. In the more restricted sense religion is limited to those realities directly and immediately connected with religious belief, worship, practice, and organization. The broader definitions can differ in a number of ways, but in my understanding the broader definition recognizes that religion in some way enters into all aspects of human existence and cannot be divorced totally from the political, cultural, social, and economic aspects of our human existence. At the very minimum one must recognize and clearly differentiate these two understandings of religion, each of which has its proper place in the discussion.

The Supreme Court itself recognizes a narrower and a broader understanding of religion. When the Court discusses questions about the establishment clause, religion is generally understood in the narrower sense. However, in other cases such as *Seeger*, dealing with conscientious objection, the Court has maintained that the concept of religion can be so interpreted that it does not necessarily even include a belief in God as such![4]

From the perspective of my understanding of Christian and Catholic theology there must also exist a broader understanding of religion. The restricted definition of religion readily allows for the distinction between the religious sphere and the secular sphere. However, such a sharp distinction and especially the separation resulting from it are unacceptable to many Christian theologians today. In fact, theologians, churches, and church people are often steadfastly insisting upon the role of the church and of faith in all aspects of our human existence.

The gospel cannot be restricted to only one small aspect of human life—the religious sphere understood in the narrow sense and confined to the realm of the private. The gospel impels Christians not only to change hearts but also to change the structures of society to serve better the needs of justice and peace. The gospel should have an influence on all aspects of the Christian life. The split between religious faith and daily human existence must be overcome. Such an understanding of the role and function of faith, of the gospel, and of the church can be found especially in recent statements of the World Council of Churches and of the Second Vatican Council.[5] The social mission of the church involving participation in the work of transforming the world and society is a constitutive dimension of the gospel itself and of the mission of the church.

Many Christians insist even more on the social mission of the church in the light of the Marxist critique that religion and Christianity are the opiate of the people. Religion tells people to put up with suffering and injustice in the present world, and their patience will be rewarded with eternal life in the future. Reacting against this criticism, many contemporary Christians have stressed the importance of the church's involvement in the struggle for justice and liberation. The gospel message of freedom affects the whole person in all aspects—personal, social, cultural, economic, and political. Perhaps the strongest apologetic for the Christian faith today is the fact that practicing Christians are concerned and trying to do something about the problem of the oppressed, the poor, and the needy.[6]

From the perspective of the American self-understanding, both definitions of religion must be retained. Theoretically the American proposition recognizes religious pluralism and proclaims that civil unity can and should exist side by side with religious pluralism. Many people who profess different religions or no religion at all join together to form a civic unity. The nonestablishment clause of the First Amendment safeguards this reality. In this respect there is a proper place for the more limited and restricted definition and understanding of religion.

However, the American system does not exclude religion or faith understood in the broader sense from affecting society. Ours is not a professedly atheistic society in which there is no room for faith and belief in God, even though some people may be atheists, and their right to such a position must be scrupulously protected and safeguarded. American democracy differs considerably from the Continental liberalism of the nineteenth century which proclaimed there was no room for religion and faith in society. Religion was relegated to a personal and private role. Our system professes the incompetency of the government and of the state in religious matters (understood in the strict sense) and protects the religious freedom of all citizens, but it still recognizes that religion in the broader sense can and should have a role in society and even in legislation and government.[7]

Especially in recent times our American experience testifies to this theoretical understanding. The two most significant social problems faced by our nation and involving government legislation and action in the last few decades have been the questions of racial discrimination and war. In both these issues the churches have contributed heavily to changing our laws and our public policy. In fact, there were a number of voices in society and in the church who condemned the churches for not being in the forefront of the movements for racial equality and for an end to the unjust war in Vietnam. There are many other issues on which religious people and churches, committed to their religious beliefs, have sought an impact on legislation and society—questions of poverty and welfare, gun control, the acceptance of the Panama Canal treaty and of the Salt II treaty, nuclear weapons and defense, nuclear power, capital punishment, women's rights, and many other such questions.

Both American theory and American practice recognize that religion, understood in the broad sense, can and should influence not only society but also government and legislation. Christian theology also argues strenuously for the involvement of individuals and churches in influencing government and the state. For these reasons I strongly oppose the contention that the Hyde Amend-

ment is unconstitutional because it legislates one religious view or because of the lobbying effort of the
Catholic Church. If this principle were accepted, faith and
the churches could no longer make a contribution to
government and legislation.

However, one must recognize that there are also illegitimate and unacceptable ways in which religion and
churches might influence government and legislation. (I
am not talking now about what might be called imprudent and therefore wrong ways. For example, one cannot
say that single-issue politics is unconstitutional, but in
my judgment it is politically imprudent and wrong.)
Think, for example, of prohibition laws or of laws against
selling contraceptives. It is necessary to have some criterion, then, to distinguish legitimate and illegitimate involvement of religion and of the churches in the political
process.

To phrase the question in terms of distinguishing
religious and nonreligious purpose is not felicitous because of the different ways in which religion can be
understood and because of the danger that religion in the
broad sense will be excluded from the sphere of influencing the state and legislation. Likewise, the criterion of
secular purpose seems to promote a dichotomy between
the secular and the religious and thereby fails to recognize
the influence religion in the broad sense of the term can
and should have. I prefer the criterion of truly political
purpose. Note that we are talking about the specific
question of the impact of religion and faith on the state,
government, and legislation and not about the broader
question of its influence on society in general.

When dealing explicitly with the question of restricting
the freedom of all people in society, there are three
principles which spell out the meaning of truly political
purpose and should guide the role of religion and of the
churches in determining what is truly political purpose.

First, the freedom of human beings is to be respected as
far as possible and curtailed only when and insofar as
necessary.

Second, the principle for state action or restriction of freedom is the public order, which is a much more restricted concept than the common good. The public order is the narrow area in which the coercive power of the state appropriately functions. There are three aspects that make up the public order—an order of justice including social justice and human rights, an order of public morality (this refers to the morality necessary for people to live together in society), and an order of public peace. The state should intervene to protect basic human rights, to promote the economic rights of all in society, and also to prevent public disturbances of the peace.

Third, any legislation involving a restriction of freedom must be good law in the sense that it is equitable and enforceable.

There can and should be much discussion about the extension and application of the three principles which are proposed here, but the basic principles supply a framework which all religious people and churches can use in discerning on what issues they try to influence the state and its laws.

Note that in these principles no mention is made of the motivation or ultimate grounding of what constitutes the threefold aspect of the public order. Some might oppose stealing on the basis of the Judeo-Christian tradition, on the grounds of Muslim teaching, or on any number of different philosophical systems. The only determining factor is the end or purpose—a truly political purpose which concretely means a demand of the public order with its threefold aspects of justice, of public morality, and of peace.

In this brief schematic presentation I have purposely tried to present only the theory and not become involved in the origin of the theory and in its application to the particular question of abortion. The theory proposed here is fundamentally that found in the Declaration on Religious Liberty of the Second Vatican Council, which itself is heavily based on the work of John Courtney Murray.[8] One important aspect has been added—the insistence on social justice as a legitimate and necessary function of government and of law. Neither Murray nor the Vatican declaration (perhaps because of the limited subject matter of religious freedom) gave enough importance to the role of the state in preserving and promoting social justice. Unfortunately, this proposal found in official Catholic documents has not always been followed even in other Catholic documents such as the Declaration on Procured Abortion issued by the Sacred Congregation for the Doctrine of the Faith in 1974.

How would I apply these principles to the issues raised by abortion? From the perspective of the morality of abortion I believe that truly individual human life is present from the fourteenth to the twenty-first day after conception, and after that time only the life of the mother or a reason commensurate with life could morally justify an abortion. Legally, in the light of the divisions in our society and on the basis of the presumption in favor of freedom found in the first principle, I have opposed efforts to overturn the 1973 Supreme Court decision by amending the Constitution. However, I defend the right of all people who believe that truly human life is present in the fetus to work to amend the Constitution because the protection of human life is the most basic right in society. The motivation or the ultimate grounding for one's decision as to when human life does begin cannot be a basis for denying the right of people with such a judgment from working for a law that protects what they believe is human life. As for public funding, I have concluded that a creative politics should be able to find a way in which tax payers opposed to abortion would not have to support it. However, if there is no other alternative, I would reluctantly accept the public funding of medically indicated abortions for the poor.[9] Yes, people can employ the same criterion and come to different conclusions on controversial issues such as abortion. But all should admit in theory and in practice that the criterion for allowing state intervention is a truly political purpose, spelled out in terms of public order and applied in the light of the presumption in favor of freedom and of the requirements of good law.

One specific question about abortion arose in the context of the 1980 elections. Cardinal Medeiros of Boston urged the defeat of candidates in the primary and general elections who had supported the legalization of abortions.[10] As mentioned above, my position accepts the present law on abortion, but Catholics and others are within their American rights and operating on the solid criterion of political purpose if they work for a constitutional amendment to overturn the present abortion law. However, in my view it is ordinarily a violation of political prudence to vote for legislators only on the basis of one issue. All the more so, a Catholic bishop should not officially call upon Catholics to act in this manner. In this case, in fact, it seems that Cardinal Medeiros acted contrary to the position proposed by the American Catholic bishops as a whole. The Catholic bishops issued a statement in November 1979, based on a previous statement made in 1976, calling for Catholics to consider a number of important issues in deciding how they should vote. The issues included abortion, arms control and disarmament, capital punishment, the economy, education, food and agricultural policy, health care, housing, human rights, mass media, and regional conflict in the world. Thus the American Catholic bishops as a whole have opposed single-issue voting.[11]

II. The Moral Majority

One of the new phenomena arising in American politics in the last few years and especially at the time of the 1980 political campaigns has been the organized efforts of conservative evangelical Christians to work for the political causes which will counter political liberalism. The question naturally arises about the legitimacy and propriety of such involvement. This discussion has made even more important the need for criteria and principles which religious groups can and should use in determining their political involvement. Too often there exists the danger of some religionists defending their own involvement in public policy questions but accusing the opposing group of violating the American understanding of the role of separation between church and state. There are a number of different groups which belong to what has been called by some the New Christian Right. Since it is impossible to describe all these different groups, our consideration will be limited to the Moral Majority, an organization headed by Dr. Jerry Falwell. The Reverend Falwell is pastor of the Thomas Road Baptist Church in Lynchburg, Virginia. Falwell is perhaps best known and most effective through the "Old-Time Gospel Hour," a Sunday religious service carried by almost 700 TV and radio stations and reaching an estimated 21 million people. Our consideration of Falwell's position will be on the basis of his book *Listen, America!*[12] The dust cover describes the Moral Majority as a "non-profit organization intended to counter political liberalism. Its aim is to mobilize at least two million Americans to work for pro-God, pro-family policies in government, so that, according to *Conservative Digest*, 'clear-cut moral choices can be offered to the American voters for the first time in decades.' "

Falwell, in keeping with his fundamentalist theology, calls his approach "a biblical plan of action" (pp. 245-254). Our country was once great but is now sick because of permissiveness and moral decay. The moral majority must work together to overcome these problems. His first chapter describes the malaise or crisis in the military, economic, and political orders. For the first time in our lifetime America is no longer the military might of the world. Economically a growing welfare system threatens our country with bankruptcy. The free-enterprise system as found in America is clearly outlined in the Book of Proverbs. Furthermore, there is a vacuum of political leadership (pp. 8-23). The concluding chapter summarizes our five major national sins—abortion, homosexuality, pornography, humanism, and the fractured family. He is strongly opposed to communism (even defending the Rhodesia of Ian Smith and South Africa), socialism, redistribution of wealth, ERA, the no-win war strategy which we pursued in Vietnam, humanism and liberalism, the Salt II Treaty, the Panama Canal Treaty, government bureacracy and intrusion into all aspects of life, especially education with laws on busing, school prayer, and regulations against Christian schools. The names most frequently cited in the book include Milton Friedman and Senator Jesse Helms.

Honesty compels me to admit that I have many differences with Dr. Falwell's approach, but it is important to recognize the different types of disagreements. It is grossly unfair to accuse Falwell of violating the American system of church and state merely because on religious grounds he advocates many proposals for legislation or public policy with which I disagree. As an American I have to recognize that he has the right to propose many of these positions even though I have my right to disagree both as an American and as a Christian believer. Three areas will be touched upon in the following discussions—my theological differences with Falwell; the question of the proper criterion governing the involvement of religious individuals and groups as well as all other individuals and groups in proposing legislation and public policy; discussion of particular issues.

Theological differences

From the perspective of Christian theology my greatest area of disagreement with Dr. Falwell centers on his understanding of the role and use of scripture. My Catholic theological tradition has justly been criticized in the past for not giving enough importance to the scriptural witness. Catholic moral theology at the present time is rightly trying to incorporate a more scripturally oriented vision and grounding to its approach. However, I am in total agreement with the traditional Catholic opposition to *sola scriptura* (the scripture alone). In my judgment the *and* in Catholic theology has been most important and points to an emphasis on mediation as the basic characteristic of the Catholic theological tradition. The Catholic tradition has recognized the importance of *and*: scripture and tradition; faith and reason; Jesus and the church. Too often in the Catholic tradition the second element has been seen as too absolute and independent of the first, but the second element in these pairs must be seen in relationship to the first. The Catholic tradition in moral theology should be criticized for not giving enough importance to the scriptures, but the scriptures are not the only source of ethical wisdom and knowledge available to the Christian. Human reason understood in the broadest possible way remains an important source of ethical wisdom and knowledge for Christian social ethics. All the human sciences of politics, economics, sociology, and others are necessary in coming to specific judgments and conclusions in the area of Christian social ethics. To incarnate Christian values and attitudes in concrete reality one needs the input of all these other sciences.

Dr. Falwell seems to indicate that his whole approach is biblical. The concluding section of his book begins with a section on "A Biblical Plan of Action." Falwell nowhere explicitly admits the need or existence of sources of wisdom for Christian social ethics other than the scriptures. However, it seems that some form of human reason in general and the interpretations of many other human sciences are involved in the very fact that he has strong convictions on such specific questions as the Panama Canal Treaty and Salt II. I do not see how it is possible to claim that there is a biblical solution to these questions without recognizing an important role for human reason and the human sciences as mediating the biblical values and message.

My understanding of the use of the scriptures in determining Christian social morality differs greatly from the approach proposed in *Listen, America!* According to Falwell "The Bible is absolutely infallible, without error in all matters pertaining to faith and practice, as well as in areas such as geography, science, history, etc." (p. 63). My approach would accept the tools of biblical criticism and the importance of hermeneutics in understanding the Bible and using its teaching in forming contemporary Christian social ethics. The hermeneutic aspect recognizes that one cannot go immediately and directly from a text embedded in one historical and cultural period to an application in possibly different historical and cultural circumstances. Think, for example, of the biblical teaching on slavery. The New Testament does not seem to oppose the institution of slavery, but today most Christian theologians would strongly oppose slavery.

Criterion of political purpose

The criterion of political purpose was proposed to guide the involvement of religion, faith, and the churches in matters of legislation and public policy. The basic thrust behind such a distinction is the fundamental and absolutely necessary distinction between the realm of Christian moral teaching and the realm of legislation and public policy. Falwell's book does not explicitly deal with this question. One can understand that a particular book cannot mention all aspects of the question. However, in the context of our religiously pluralistic society Falwell and other leaders of the so-called New Christian Right must expressly deal with these questions.

Falwell explictly recognizes and upholds the separation of church and state, but he claims such an understanding does not mean a government devoid of God and the Bible (p. 53). I too can agree with that understanding in general, but it would be helpful for Falwell to develop this relationship with as much precision as possible. Our author's staunch support for the nation of Israel and his prayer for God's continuing blessing on this miracle also indicate that he accepts the separation of church and state (pp. 107-113). However, there are emphases in the book which can raise some questions about his acceptance of religious pluralism and the separation of church and state. The major thesis of the book maintains that America is suffering from moral decay and permissiveness, with the root cause in sin. Before there can be a revival, there must be an awareness and conviction of the problem of sin (p. 68). The answer to every one of our nations' dilemmas is a spiritual one. We as a nation must acknowledge God as our creator and Jesus Christ as the savior of mankind. Such an acknowledgment will turn our nation around economically and in every other way (p. 81). The book contains some startling statements, such as: "If a person is not a Christian, he is inherently a failure" (p. 62). Since nothing is said explicitly to the contrary, one could be left with the impression that the function of law and politics is to assist in and even legislate totally in accord with this view of spiritual renewal. Such statements come close to identifying the unity of the City of God with the unity of the City of Man. At the very minimum Falwell must deal more explicitly and precisely with this question of religious pluralism in America and the distinction between church and state.

There is no discussion in Falwell's book on the distinction between morality and legality. Such a distinction is basic to any recognition of the need for determining a criterion to direct and justify religious involvement in legislation and public policy. The frequent citations of biblical texts on particular issues can readily give the impression that one can move directly from the level of the revealed morality of the Bible to the level of the political and legal. A real difference between morality and legality must be recognized especially in the matter of what is often called private morality. Here, as pointed out above, the first rule of jurisprudence calls for as much freedom as possible and as little restraint as necessary. Falwell must deal more explicitly and precisely with these questions.

Particular issues

In terms of political discourse the central focus of my disagreements with Falwell is on many specific issues, as illustrated in the description of his position, which he supports on the basis of biblical warrants. I disagree on most of these issues both in regard to the substance of the issue and with the contention that these are Christian or biblical approaches. My differences with Falwell are not based on the accusation that he is violating the spirit or letter of the American separation of church and state by supporting these issues in the name of the Bible. It is impossible to discuss all these particular issues, but I will mention three very significant areas of disagreement—the use of military force, the distribution of the goods of creation, and the role of America in the plan of God.

Falwell decries the decline in our military power, our appeasement vis-à-vis communism, our attempts at disarmament, and our no-win war policies. He justifies the use of the sword by government as revenging and executing God's wrath on those who do evil (e.g., p. 98). Much has been written about the Christian and biblical approach to peace and war. At the very minimum Falwell gives no attention to the many sayings attributed to Jesus (he would have to maintain they are literally the statements of the historical Jesus) about peace and mercy. On the basis of the scriptures some Christians are convinced pacificists. Even those who have accepted war, as in the theory of just war, stress that war is always a last resort, and there are limitations on the ways in which war can be waged. Falwell's approach to military might and strength seems to be opposed to the approaches taken by most of the Christian tradition.

Falwell strongly defends free enterprise, laissez-faire capitalism, and a limited and decentralized government (p. 72). "The free-enterprise system is clearly outlined in the Book of Proverbs in the Bible. Jesus Christ made it clear that the work ethic was a part of his plan for man. Ownership of property is biblical. Competition in business is biblical. Ambitious and successful business management is clearly outlined as part of God's plan for His people" (p. 13). Many Christians would rightly disagree with some of the above statements and emphases. Again, it is impossible to develop a full Christian approach to the economic and political orders. However, in my judgment the very first thing that a Christian must say about worldly goods is that the goods of creation exist to serve the needs of all. This is the understanding found in recent documents of the World Council of Churches and of conciliar and papal Catholic social teaching. Pope Paul VI in his encyclical *Populorum progressio* asserted, "All other rights whatsoever, including those of property and of free commerce, are to be subordinated to this principle."[13]

Although Falwell finds decay and weaknesses in contemporary America, he basically sees America as God's chosen people. "I love America because, she, above all the nations of the world, has honored the principles of the Bible. America has been great because she has been good" (p. 263). Falwell speaks out "against Godless communism which would seek to destroy the work of Christ that is going out from this base of America" (p. 106). Falwell too readily identifies the cause of the United States with the cause of God and God's plan. The Judaeo-Christian tradition has always nourished within itself a prophetic aspect and an eschatological aspect which calls on all believers to reexamine their own lives, causes, and nations. Arrogance and not biblical teaching is the source of the identification of America with the cause of God.

In conclusion, I agree with Falwell that faith and religion should not be excluded from our laws and public policy. However, it is incumbent upon him in the future to spell out more clearly what is the relationship between the two. I have attempted to do so with the criterion of political purpose and the three principles which spell out the meaning and applications of political purpose. Falwell must clearly distinguish between morality and legality in what are often called questions of private morality. In the meantime in the area of private morality he is vulnerable to the charge of not distinguishing properly between the role of the church and of the state. On most of the specific issues of public policy which Falwell endorses I do not dispute his right as an American to propose such positions and even to base them on his understanding of the Christian faith. My disagreement with the founder of the Moral Majority is on the substantive positions he takes and the Christian and biblical warrants he gives for those positions. I think he is wrong both with regard to most of his positions and with regard to his claim that these represent Christian or biblical teaching.

This study has dealt with the problem of the relationship between faith or religion and American political life. Two emotionally charged issues have been considered. There is always the danger in such an atmosphere of accusing those who disagree with my position of violating the American principle of the separation of church and state, while at times I use religious reasons to support the public policy I agree with. There is need for consistency, discipline, and restraint in our argumentation. The criterion of political purpose determines what constitutes a legitimate involvement of religious ideas into the political arena. In the light of this criterion it is legitimate for people on the basis of their religious and philosophical principles to work for legislation which forbids abortion or the public funding of abortion. Note, however, that for a number of reasons I do not favor such action. Dr. Falwell needs to explain more clearly how he understands the relationship between religious beliefs and principles and political life in our country. Although on many issues such as defense, military, and economic policies his religiously grounded positions do not violate the American understanding of the relationship between church and state, nevertheless, in my judgment his positions are often erroneous. Hopefully these considerations might contribute to a better understanding of the relationship between religion and politics and to a more precise and accurate public discourse.

NOTES

1. Copies of the brief can be obtained from Center for Constitutional Rights, 853 Broadway, New York, New York 10003.

2. *Harris* v. *McRae*, 48 USLW 4941, June 30, 1980. For different reactions to the decision of the Supreme Court, see John T. Noonan, Jr., "The Supreme Court and Abortion:

Upholding Constitutional Principles," *The Hastings Center Report* 10, 6 (December 1980), 14-16; David Mechanic, "The Supreme Court and Abortion: Sidestepping Social Realities," *The Hastings Report* 10, 6 (December 1980), 17-19.

3. *Committee for Public Education* v. *Nyquist*, 413 U.S. 756, 773 (1973).

4. *United States* v. *Seeger*, 380 U.S. 163 (1965). For a discussion of the question of selective conscientious objection, see John A. Rohr, *Prophets Without Honor: Public Policy and the Selective Conscientious Objector* (New York: Abingdon, 1971).

5. Paul Bock, *In Search of a Responsible World Society: The Social Teaching of the World Council of Churches* (Philadelphia: Westminster, 1974); *Renewing the Earth: Catholic Documents on Peace, Justice and Liberation*, eds. David J. O'Brien and Thomas A. Shannon (Garden City, New York: Doubleday Image Book, 1977).

6. Such themes are often found in contemporary political and liberation theology. See Dorothy Soelle, *Political Theology* (Philadelphia: Fortress Press, 1974); Gustavo Gutierrez, *A Theology of Liberation* (Maryknoll, New York: Orbis Books, 1972).

7. John Courtney Murray, *We Hold These Truths: Catholic Reflections on the American Proposition* (New York: Sheed and Ward, 1960).

8. John Courtney Murray, *The Problem of Religious Freedom* (Westminster, Md.: Newman Press, 1965), pp. 40-45.

9. Charles E. Curran, *Ongoing Revision in Moral Theology* (Notre Dame, Indiana: Fides/Claretian Publications, 1975); pp. 107-143; *Transition and Tradition in Moral Theology* (Notre Dame, Indiana: University of Notre Dame Press, 1979), pp. 207-250.

10. "Abortion and the Elections: Cardinal Medeiros," *Origins: N.C. Documentary Service* 10 (September 25, 1980), 239.

11. United States Catholic Conference Administrative Board, "Political Responsibility: Choices for the 1980s," *Origins: N.C. Documentary Service* 9 (November 15, 1979), 349-355. See also *Origins: N.C. Documentary Service* 6 (September 30, 1976), 236.

12. Jerry Falwell, *Listen, America!* (Garden City, New York: Doubleday, 1980). Page numbers in the subsequent paragraphs will refer to this book.

13. Pope Paul VI, *Populorum Progressio*, par. 22, in *Renewing the Earth*, p. 320.

Index

AAUP, *see* American Association of University Professors

abortion, xiv, 84, 124, 127, 136, 165n, 209, 210, 215, 216, 217, 255; abortion legislation, 209, 210, 214; Hyde Amendment, 210, 213f; public funding of, 209, 225

academe, setting for moral theology, xii, 11, 12, 13, 16, 25, 26, 68

academic due process, 14-15, 25, 31n

academic freedom, xii, 7, 11, 12-15, 16, 20, 21, 25, 29n, 31n; and Catholic universities, 11, 12, 15-17, 19, 21, 22, 26, 28, 29n, 30n; and Roman Catholic theology, theologians, 11, 22, 25, 26; and *Sapientia christiana*, 11, 27, 28

acedia, see sloth

Address to the Fourth International Congress of Catholic Doctors, 1949, 120, 122

addresses, papal, 114, 137n; *see also* individual addresses listed by title

adoption, 123

aging, xiii, 93-108, 109n, 110n, 155

AID, *see* artificial insemination

AIH, *see* artificial insemination

Alexander III, Pope, 25

allocutions, papal, 114, 115, 120, 137n; *see also* individual allocutions listed by title

Altizer, Thomas J.J., 168n

American Academic Freedom Project, 15

American Association of Retired Persons, 109n

American Association of University Professors, 13, 14, 16, 29n; with American Council on Education, *1940 Statement of Principles on Academic Freedom and Tenure*, 14, 15, 16, 31n; *A Declaration of Principles, 1915*, 13, 15; *1958 Statement on Procedural Standards in Faculty Dismissal Proceedings*, 14; *1976 Recommended Institutional Regulations on Academic Freedom and Tenure*, 14

American Council on Education, 13; *Conference Statement on Academic Freedom and Tenure*, 13; *see also* American Association of University Professors